Fun & Fabulous Tops to Sew

10 Easy Designs for the Totally Cool Beginner

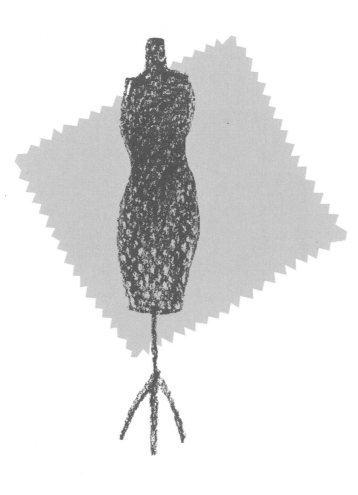

Fun & Fabulous Tops to Sew
10 Easy Designs for the Totally Cool Beginner

Valerie Van Arsdale Shrader

LARK BOOKS

A Division of Sterling Publishing Co., Inc.
New York

ART DIRECTOR:
Megan Kirby

COVER DESIGNER:
Barbara Zaretsky

ASSISTANT EDITOR:
Rebecca Guthrie

ASSOCIATE ART DIRECTOR:
Shannon Yokeley

ART PRODUCTION ASSISTANT:
Jeff Hamilton

EDITORIAL ASSISTANCE:
Delores Gosnell

PHOTOGRAPHER:
Stewart O'Shields

ART INTERN:
Ardyce E. Alspach

EDITORIAL INTERN:
Sue Stigleman

ILLUSTRATOR:
Susan McBride

Acknowledgments

I love to sew! I'm so glad it's cool again.

Thanks to the creative sewers who made the garments for this book; please read about them on page 107. Photographer Stewart O'Shields made beautiful images of the tops, and the following businesses in Asheville, North Carolina, were gracious hosts for our photo shoots: Diggin' Art; Café on the Square (cafeonthesquare@bellsouth .net); Harvest Records (harvestrecords@ mail.com); Jerusalem Garden Café; Bobo Gallery; The L.O.F.T. (info@ loftofasheville.com); Beauty Parade; and Limones Restaurant. And Aimee Hills, the scooter was awesome!

Lastly, thanks to the folks at Lark Books, especially design whiz Megan Kirby, the art director for *Fun & Fabulous Tops*, and organizational guru Rebecca Guthrie, the assistant editor.

Library of Congress Cataloging-in-Publication Data

Shrader, Valerie Van Arsdale.
  Fun & fabulous tops to sew: 10 easy designs for the totally cool beginner/ Valerie Van Arsdale Shrader.-- 1st ed.
      p. cm.
  Includes index.
  ISBN 1-57990-803-9 (hardcover)
  1. Blouses. 2. Jackets. 3. Dressmaking. 4. Fancy work. I. Title.
TT545.S5674 2006
646.4'35--dc22

                                    2005034825

10 9 8 7 6 5 4 3 2 1

First Edition

Published by Lark Books, A Division of
Sterling Publishing Co., Inc.
387 Park Avenue South, New York, N.Y. 10016

Text © 2006, Lark Books
Photography © 2006, Lark Books unless otherwise noted

Distributed in Canada by Sterling Publishing,
c/o Canadian Manda Group, 165 Dufferin Street
Toronto, Ontario, Canada M6K 3H6

Distributed in the United Kingdom by GMC Distribution Services,
Castle Place, 166 High Street, Lewes, East Sussex, England BN7 1XU

Distributed in Australia by Capricorn Link (Australia) Pty Ltd.,
P.O. Box 704, Windsor, NSW 2756 Australia

If you have questions or comments about this book, please contact:
Lark Books
67 Broadway
Asheville, NC 28801
(828) 253-0467

Manufactured in China

ISBN 13: 978-1-57990-803-4
ISBN 10: 1-57990-803-9

For information about custom editions, special sales, premium and corporate purchases, please contact Sterling Special Sales Department at 800-805-5489 or specialsales@sterlingpub.com.

Contents

Introduction

Top depression. We've all had it at one time or another, so you'll probably recognize the symptoms. It starts with a to-die-for skirt or the best-fitting pair of jeans you've ever owned. There's usually a date or a party thrown into the mix, too. So—what to wear with that great skirt or fantastic jeans?

Absolutely nothing in the closet will do. *Nothing.* Not an option. You could order from a catalog, but what if you don't like it when it comes? No time to shop for a replacement. A trip to your favorite boutique yields nothing you could afford without winning the lottery. Hmmm. Here's an idea—why don't you make your own fabulous top, in the perfect color, fabric, and design to complement that luscious skirt or those heart-stopping jeans? A radical idea, isn't it? I'll even teach you how to sew, right here in this book.

Wait. I sense resistance. You're not *afraid* to learn to sew, are you? Of course not—you ride the subway every day, and you're as talented, creative, and smart as they come. Is it the dorky stuff you had to make in home ec class? I promise you that *Fun & Fabulous Tops* are just that—modern designs made of totally gorgeous fabric with thoroughly hip details such as exposed raw edges and funky embellishment. Sewing is as cool as it gets today. In fact, sewing has had an extreme makeover, because you no longer have to tidy up everything and hide the seams—leave the hem unfinished if you want, and hey, put the seams on the outside if you dare. Sewing has been liberated!

This blouse rocks!

Now that I've convinced you that a great top is worth learning to sew for, I promise to make the learning curve as gentle as possible. We'll make 10 great tops, starting with the simplest style you can imagine—a linen tank with simple ribbon trim—and work our way up to easy jackets that look just like the ones you saw on the runway during Fashion Week. We'll only talk about what you need to know to make a top, and nothing more—none of that tailoring stuff that makes your eyes glaze over. We'll go through the whole process, starting with choosing a pattern, because once you understand all the information in a pattern, you'll be ready to shop for scrumptious fabric to make that perfect top. After we discuss fabric, we'll get

right to the sewing, and we've got tons of photos to illustrate the important steps along the way.

And after you've made your first fabulous top, I'll bet you'll be hooked, because you'll see how easy it is to create your own wardrobe. Now, you decide on all the details—the design, the fabric, and the embellishment. Your tops, blouses, and jackets become a personal artistic statement. It's all about *you!*

To make a long introduction short (and get on with the book), I promise that I can, and *will*, cure your top depression. I'm living proof. Let's get started now—turn the page, please.

Guide to Making Fabulous Tops

Cute design, lovely fabric, and a great day of shopping, too!

When you're suffering from top depression, how do you feel? You want a stylish design in a luscious fabric, right? These two elements, the design and the fabric, are the key to making a top you'll love. Deciding which comes first—the fabric or the pattern—depends on your mindset. But since this book is all about fabulous tops, let's start with the pattern, the actual design you'll use to make your first top.

If you're new to sewing (remember, you've got to learn how if you want to make a top), it helps to understand the information in a pattern and how the kind of blouse you want to make will be affected by your fabric choice. You become the designer *and* the creator of your wardrobe when you sew, so there's more freedom than you have when you shop for a top—no more liking the style, but settling for a so-so color. Now you choose which patterns to use, which details to include, and which fabric to splurge on. You're no longer at the mercy of ready-to-wear and you can really apply your personality to your wardrobe.

Since I'm a fabric junkie and an experienced sewer, I tend to be attracted to fabrics first and then find a pattern. But I think it helps the new (or reincarnated) sewer to understand patterns first, and then choose the right fabric. So let's begin by talking about patterns, and then fabric. We'll deal with that sewing stuff later (after a nice latte), when we go through the process of making a top in detail. I promise not to overload you with information about sewing that you don't need and probably won't ever use; we're trying to keep it as simple as we can. Finally, we'll get right down to it and make 10 cool tops—including some blouses and simple jackets, too. All the information you'll find in this section of the book will be the foundation for the actual projects themselves, so refer to it as often as you need to.

Pick a pattern

You'll be pleased and probably relieved to know that a top doesn't have to be difficult to be the perfect expression of your creativity. In *Fun & Fabulous Tops,* you'll learn all the steps to create beautiful tops—but it's okay, we won't tackle everything at once. Each of the 10 projects in the book offers skills in a progressive manner, so you can create an entire wardrobe of tops and expand your repertoire of skills with each project. The patterns we've chosen use basic techniques, but also add some contemporary details such as ribbon embellishments, edgy construction, and creative stitching. Patterns (and all that stuff inside) sometimes seem intimidating, but actually the pattern is the key to the top of your dreams. (Don't let those jeans be lonely for too long.) Let's talk about patterns in general terms now; we'll find out how to actually use them when we Learn to Sew! on page 23.

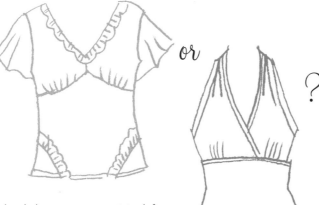

or

?

Trying to decide between patterns? Look for details you want to include in your top, such as sleeves or neckline style.

Fabric shops offer a variety of catalogs from the major pattern companies. Each company issues a new catalog seasonally, just as designers continually produce new collections, so you can be sure to find current designs as well as classic silhouettes. The pattern catalogs are like Fashion Week in a book! When you visit your local fabric shop, look through the tops sections of the various catalogs for all the possibilities. When you find a style that appeals to you, read through the information about the design. Generally, you'll find out how much fabric you need, what type of fabric is recommended for that style, and which other notions (zippers, buttons, etc.) you'll need to make the top. Most patterns offer variations on the basic design, sometimes as many as six in one envelope. (More for your money!) The variations are usually labeled with letters (View A, Top B, etc.).

A typical pattern envelope

STYLE, FIT, AND CONSTRUCTION DETAILS.
This describes the kind of top you'll be making.

PATTERN NAME AND NUMBER.
Here's the top you found in
the pattern catalog.

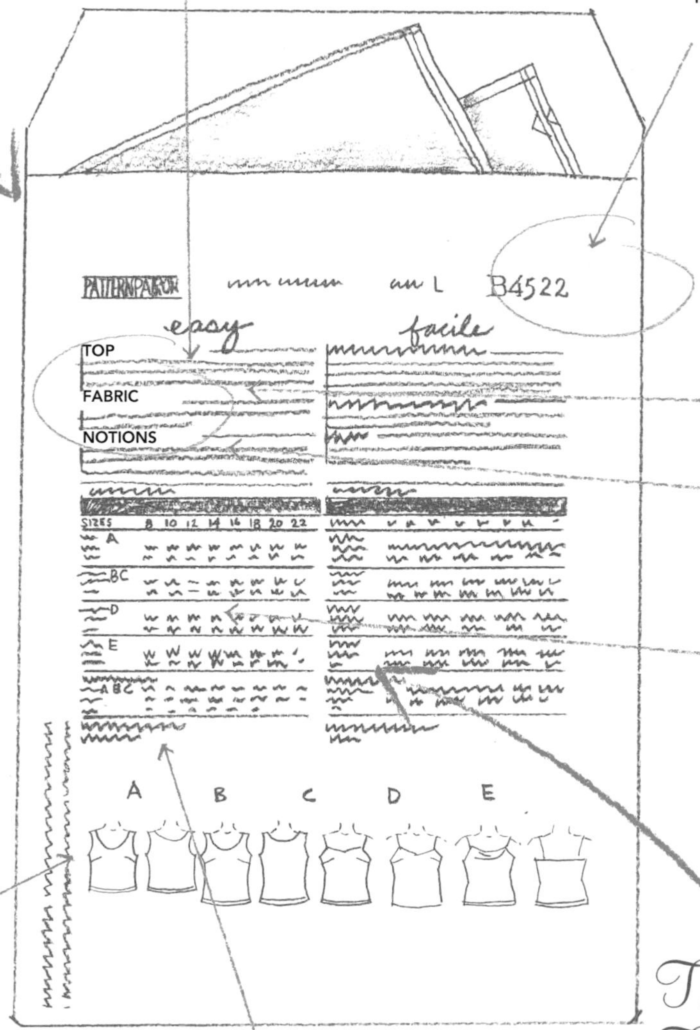

PATTERNPARLOR   *easy*   *au L*   **B4522**

facile

TOP

FABRIC

NOTIONS

FABRIC SUGGESTIONS.
Choose from this list of
suggested fabrics.

NOTIONS. In addition to the
pattern and the fabric,
here's the other stuff you
need to make your top.

SIZES   8   10   12   14   16   18   20   22

A

BC

D

E

ABC

FABRIC REQUIREMENTS.
Follow the columns below
your size to find out how
much fabric you need.

A   B   C   D   E

VARIATIONS. Here
are all the cute tops
you can make from
this pattern.

FINISHED MEASUREMENTS.
Some of the measurements for the
finished top will be listed here.

*This side is usually in
French. Très chic, non?*

Outside the pattern envelope

Now, after you find an irresistible design in the catalog, study the pattern envelope itself for even more information. Most of the patterns used in this book were labeled "Easy" or "Fast" or something similar. Until you've gained some skills and confidence (which won't be long), stick to patterns that are similarly labeled. Refer to the illustration on the opposite page as we talk about what you'll learn from the pattern envelope.

STYLE, FIT, AND CONSTRUCTION DETAILS. It may say something like, "Pullover tank top in two lengths" or "Unlined jacket with collar variations." This listing gives you specific information about the style of the top and its construction.

You should also know about *ease*. Patterns include varying amounts of wearing ease and design ease. Wearing ease is the additional sizing included in your top so you can move in it, while design ease is added to achieve a particular silhouette. The terms you see on your pattern envelope, such as "loose-fitting" or "fitted," refer to design ease. The amount of ease you prefer is personal, so if you like body-hugging clothes, don't buy a pattern for a loose-fitting garment. You'll be disappointed in the fit.

NOTIONS. Patterns list all the additional items that you need to finish the project, such as "1 yard of ½-inch elastic" or "7-inch zipper, 3 yards of ¾-inch-wide ribbon trim."

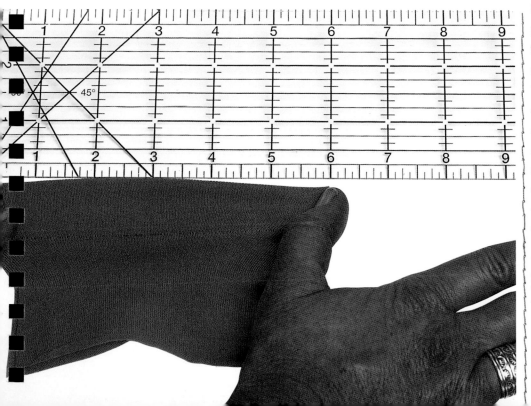

FABRIC SUGGESTIONS. Most companies list a range of fabrics that will be suitable for each design, including things like "silks and silk types, cotton and cotton blends, and lightweight denim." Some patterns are designed for stretch knits only, so be sure to take note of whether you need a stretchy fabric for your top. The pattern will tell you so.

To make sure your knit fabric is suitable, you'll usually have to stretch it from *here* to *there* along the edge of the pattern. A typical example is like this—stretching 4 inches of folded fabric to 6 inches.

We'll spend more time talking about fabric in just a few minutes, but the important thing to understand now is that you'll have lots of appropriate fabric choices for each design.

FABRIC REQUIREMENTS. You'll find out how much fabric you need to make your chosen blouse.

FINISHED MEASUREMENTS. The extent of this information varies among pattern companies, but generally you'll find the bust measurements and finished length. Note that the bust measurements will differ from actual body measurements because they include ease, as we just discussed. (You were paying attention, weren't you?)

Inside the pattern envelope

The envelope contains the pattern pieces themselves, printed on tissue paper, and the instructions for the top. Don't be overwhelmed by the information inside, because it's all presented in small digestible bits. We should be thankful that the pattern companies have figured out how to give us so much useful stuff in such a tidy package.

PATTERN PIECES. Modern patterns generally contain more than one size, and all the pieces for the top will be printed on one or more large sheets of tissue paper. When you've identified your size and the style you want to make (Top B, let's say), refer to the instruction sheet for a key to tell you which pieces you need to use.

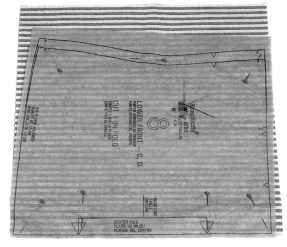

Each pattern piece is important to your top.

INSTRUCTIONS. You'll find cutting layouts, which illustrate how to place the pattern pieces on the fabric and cut them out. You'll also have sewing directions, which give you step-by-step instructions on making your top. There are also some general sewing tips to supplement the instructions; we're going to cover this basic information here, too. Read over the instructions *completely* before you begin making your blouse or jacket so you understand the sequence of its construction. Please.

Which size?

You probably won't admit it, but I bet this is the real reason you've avoided learning to sew. Pattern companies don't use the same sizing that apparel manufacturers use. Take a deep breath before I tell you that you may need to buy a pattern that's two, three, or possibly *four* sizes larger than what you'd buy in ready-to-wear. I hear you moaning now, but think through this logically; it's just a number, after all. The system of sizing the pattern companies use is simply different.

To demonstrate this, here's a comparison of measurements:

	MAJOR PATTERN COMPANY	MAJOR APPAREL COMPANY
Bust	32½	32½
Waist	25	25
Hip	34½	35
Size	**10**	**2**

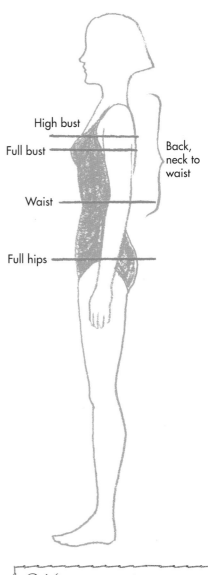

High bust

Full bust

Back, neck to waist

Waist

Full hips

Amazing, isn't it? This, sweetie, is a practice called *vanity sizing*: the garment industry cuts its clothing generously while putting a teeny little size on the tag. Neither be fooled nor disappointed by this trickery.

To make sure your top fits, measure yourself accurately according to the illustration at the right. Buy the size that most closely matches your bust measurement, unless there's more than two inches between your bust and your high bust. If the difference is greater than two inches, use your high bust measurement to determine your size. (The relationship of these measurements involves your cup size.) If you're trying to decide between two sizes, get the larger one. (Sorry about that.) Now, forget about the garment industry and its sizing—you're making your own tops now.

When you take your measurements, wear normal undies. The tape should be snug, but not tight. Don't cheat!

Choose your fabric

Okay, you've found a pattern with a great design. You love it! Now the search for fabric begins. This is the exciting part of making a top, because your project starts to get real when you can feel the fabric. Imagine that you're in Paris and you could have any blouse you wanted; making your own blouse is absolutely no different, because you *can* have anything you want. Spend some quality time looking for fabric. If you don't like the color, or the print, or the drape of the fabric, you won't like the top. Remember that your pattern envelope will offer you a variety of fabrics that are suitable for your project, so be sure to choose one of the types that's suggested.

Fabric basics

I won't bore you with lots of information about fabric, because I suspect you'll become entranced with it and learn a lot on your own. (I've already cast the spell. Remember I have a love affair with fabric.) But a little general information is definitely in order. Fabrics can be woven or knit, and are made of fibers of various origins. Since you're into clothes, you probably already have a basic knowledge of the different types of fabric and what they're made from: the natural fibers, such as cotton, linen, wool, and silk; and the synthetic fibers, like polyester, acrylic, and nylon. (Thank you, chemists!) Rayon straddles these two categories, as it's synthesized from wood pulp; it's manmade, yet from a natural source. Other synthetic fabrics are made from sources such as petroleum products, and many fabrics are blends of natural and synthetic fibers.

If a fabric is woven, its weave gives it specific characteristics. Satin, velvet, twill, and so on all describe the structure of the fabric, and not its fiber content. Velvet can be made from silk, cotton, or polyester, for example. But when you're learning to make a top, the properties of the fabric (drape, texture, weight, etc.) are just as important as the fiber content. As long as it hangs the way it's supposed to, you have some flexibility as to what you can use. These are the parameters the pattern companies use when they suggest a range of fabrics for a specific design. Isn't that thoughtful of them? I think so.

Knit fabrics—the stuff your favorite tees are made of—aren't woven, but are formed through the looping of yarn. (If you know how to knit, it's pretty much the same process. Sorta.) Knits stretch and conform to the body, unlike woven fabrics. We've used a couple of knit fabrics in *Fun & Fabulous Tops,* and we'll give you some tips about sewing with these fabrics as we go along.

An awesome fabric + a simple pattern = a great top.

Will it work?

So how do you know whether your fabric will drape properly? Well, you can tell a lot from fabric by touching and manipulating it before you buy it. (Don't worry. The folks in the fabric stores are used to people fondling fabric.) In all seriousness, you really must feel the material, as you'll be working with it and wearing it—is it smooth? Thin or heavy? Stiff or soft? Unfold a length of fabric from the bolt and observe how it hangs. If you want a top with a little flounce that drapes just so, you need a lightweight fabric; if you want a crisp silhouette, a medium-weight linen might be just perfect.

Each bolt of fabric will be labeled with its fiber content, its width, its price, and occasionally its laundering requirements. Before you buy it, be sure to ask about laundering the fabric, so you understand how you must care for your top after you've made it. Washable fabrics need to be preshrunk before being sewn, which simply means laundering them according to the manufacturer's recommendations before you start.

For a first top, consider using a medium-weight cotton, because it handles and washes well, it's durable, and it's easy to sew. We used a wide variety of fabrics in *Fun & Fabulous Tops,* including cotton, linen, silk, wool, and synthetic blends, so you can see how diverse your choices will be. But don't get carried away—while slinky charmeuse or flimsy chiffon might be beautiful, they're a little more difficult to handle than cotton or linen and thus not well suited for a first top project. (Now, a second or third top? That's a different story.)

Simply put, don't use a fabric that feels slippery for your first blouse, because it's likely to scoot around when you cut it or sew with it, and you're likely to get discouraged. A common mistake that beginners make is choosing a luscious fabric that requires a certain degree of sewing experience to properly handle. Believe me when I tell you that there are beautiful cottons available that will make your first top a happy experience.

FOX
MODEL
FORM

COLLAPSIBLE

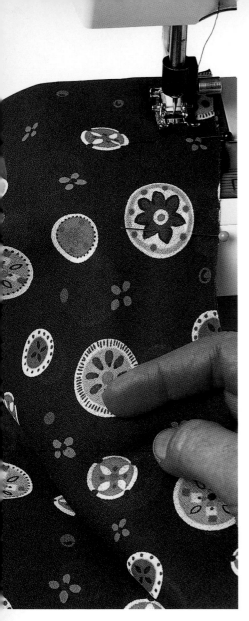

With fabric like this, you'll want to sew all day!

Meet the Sewing Machine

The next step is to develop a meaningful relationship with your sewing machine, since it's the tool that will free you from top depression. Give it a friendly little pat and let's get to know it better. Later, when we Learn to Sew! on page 23, we'll discuss some of its functions in greater detail. I love my sewing machine! I really do.

How it works

This fantastic invention creates a lockstitch when the thread from the needle (on top of the machine) and the thread from the bobbin (inside the machine) loop together in the fabric. This happens a gazillion times per minute when you sew. (Aren't you glad you don't have to do it by hand? I sure am.) That's the long, the short, and the zigzag of it.

Although machines share common characteristics, they vary by manufacturer. When I keep referring you to your own machine's manual, I'm not trying to ignore your needs; it's because there are some subtle yet important differences between machines that might confuse you. For instance, the thread on my machine disappears inside for part of its journey—yours might not. My bobbin winds on the front of the machine—yours might be on top. I have a pressure foot dial, but you might have a lever. Despite that rambling disclaimer, let's have a go at some general information anyway.

See the illustration on the opposite page: a typical machine has a spool (or spools) for the thread; controls for stitch width, stitch length, thread tension, and presser foot pressure (say that three times fast); a handwheel; a take-up lever; tension disks; a presser foot lever; thread guides; a bobbin winder; a needle; a presser foot; feed dogs; a needle plate; and a bobbin. All of these things furiously work together to create the little lockstitch

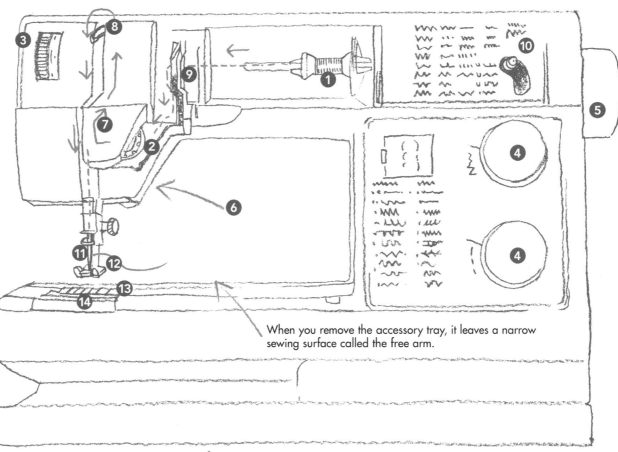

When you remove the accessory tray, it leaves a narrow sewing surface called the free arm.

A sewing machine overview

1. The spool holds the thread.

2. This dial adjusts the thread tension; turn it in tiny increments.

3. Adjust the pressure of the presser foot with this dial.

4. These dials adjust stitch selection, including width and length.

5. The handwheel revolves when you sew, and you can turn it by hand for precision work.

6. The presser foot lever (hiding in the back) lifts the presser foot and engages the tension disks. Remember to put it in the down position when you sew! But *lift* the presser foot when you thread your machine.

7. The tension disks, tucked inside the machine, regulate the movement of the thread.

8. The take-up lever carries the thread while the machine is sewing, pulling the exact amount it needs for each stitch. If this lever isn't threaded properly, an unsightly gob of thread will appear on your fabric.

9. The thread guides move the thread through the machine in an orderly fashion.

10. The bobbin winder winds the thread on the bobbin. (It's not named very creatively, is it?)

11. The needle pierces the fabric and creates a stitch when its thread is looped together with the thread from the bobbin. Use the right size needle for your fabric, and use a new needle for each project.

12. The presser foot keeps the fabric snug against the feed dogs, the little serrated thingies that move the fabric as you sew.

13. The needle plate is the metal surface through which the needle grabs the bobbin thread. It has handy guidelines for seam allowances.

14. The bobbin is wound with thread and lives inside the machine. The looping of the thread from the spool with the thread from the bobbin forms the basic lockstitch.

that makes the top that cures top depression. Most modern machines have a detachable accessory tray that's part of the sewing surface; when it's removed, a narrow sewing surface called a *free arm* remains. The free arm lets you stitch around narrow openings like cuffs.

In case you could have possibly forgotten (!), your sewing machine manual is the best source of information for your particular model. It will have detailed information about threading the machine; winding the bobbin; adjusting stitch width and length; and selecting any specialty stitches. Read through the manual thoroughly before you begin to make your top and practice stitching to familiarize yourself with the operation of your machine. It will be fun!

Use the right needle

There's no great mystery to choosing the proper needle for your top. The three major types are sharps, for use on finely woven fabrics; ballpoints, for knits; and universal points, for all-purpose sewing on both knits and woven fabrics. Needles come in different sizes, with the smaller numbers for use on lightweight fabrics and the larger numbers for heavyweight material. They're marked in both European (60, 70, etc.) and American (10, 12, and so on) sizes; which number comes first depends on the manufacturer. A universal point in the medium range (70/10 or 80/12, for instance) will suit most of the fabric used in this book. For the easy way out, try this: when you buy your fabric, smile brightly at the clerk and ask for a recommendation.

Use the right presser foot

The presser foot is the gismo that keeps the fabric secure against the feed dogs; the feed dogs are the gismos that move the fabric along as you sew. There are lots of specialized presser feet designed to perform specific tasks, but we keep it simple in this book by using only two: a general presser foot that allows both straight and zigzag stitching, and the zipper foot, which lets you stitch close to the zipper when you're installing it. That handy manual of yours will instruct you on changing the presser feet.

Got Sewing Machine?

If you already have a sewing machine, you're ready to make a top. But, please hear this: The machine is really, really important, because if it doesn't operate properly, you won't be able to sew successfully. And you won't make any fabulous tops.

1 You don't have to spend a ton of money to get a perfectly good entry-level sewing machine. But you really should go to a dealer and test-drive before you buy. Sew over different thicknesses of fabric, thread it yourself, wind the bobbin, check out the stitch selection, make a buttonhole—dealers expect and welcome this level of scrutiny from their customers. Many dealers offer an introductory class after you've purchased a machine.

2 If you buy a used machine, insist on that test-drive, too. Stitching can look dreadfully wonky when there's actually not much wrong (maybe just a tension adjustment on the bobbin), but then again, maybe that poor machine has been abused. Have a reputable dealer inspect it before you plunk down your hard-earned cash. Make sure that you have a complete operating manual, too.

3 If you borrow a machine, please don't make the mistake of hauling a dusty machine out of someone's attic and thinking it will sew beautifully. Maybe it will, but probably it won't; sewing machines need to be tuned up regularly, just like cars. They work awfully hard, and they accumulate lots of dust from fabric and thread. (This dust migrates into the screwiest places, too.) Get a proper introduction from the machine's owner (do a lot of the same things I suggest when you're shopping for a machine) and have the owner point out its important features. Don't forget to borrow that manual, also. (As if!)

Gather the
Tools and Supplies

In addition to the sewing machine, you need to gather up a few other tools and materials before you begin your first top. All of these items are readily available at any fabric shop.

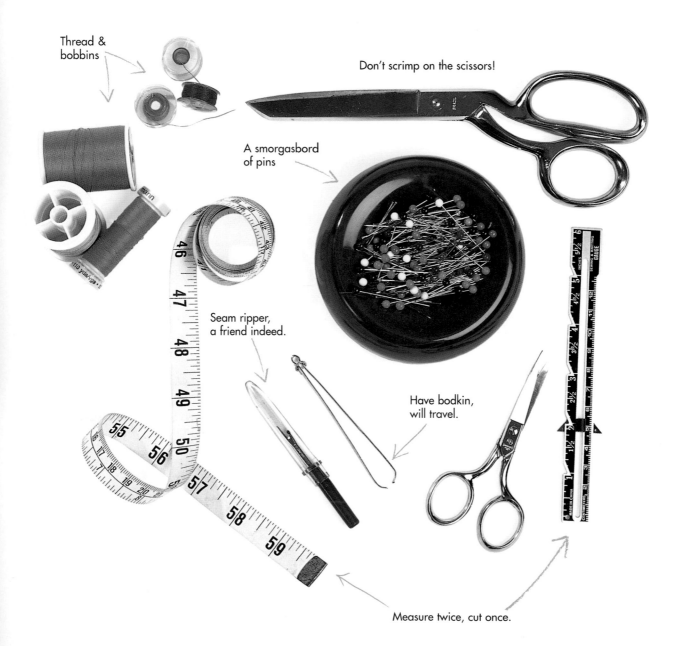

Thread & bobbins

Don't scrimp on the scissors!

A smorgasbord of pins

Seam ripper, a friend indeed.

Have bodkin, will travel.

Measure twice, cut once.

SCISSORS. If you invest in only one quality item for making tops, I suggest a good pair of 7- or 8-inch dressmaker's bent-handled shears. The design of bent-handled shears allows the fabric to remain flat, so it doesn't shift while you're cutting. A pair of sewing scissors, say 4 to 5 inches long, is perfect for other cutting tasks, such as trimming seams. Buy the best scissors you can afford, because they'll be your friend forever. I still use my grandmother's sewing scissors, which are at least 30 (if not 40) years old.

Though you should use dressmaker's shears to cut out your top, a pair of pinking shears is handy to finish seams. And they're cute, too.

SEAM RIPPER. Change is inevitable, and so are mistakes. Use a seam ripper to remove stitches that displease you.

MEASURING TOOLS. If the only measuring tool you had were a tape measure, you could certain-ly make a blouse. But a couple of other gadgets will be useful, too: a clear ruler helps while cutting out fabric, and a sewing gauge is a nifty little tool that has a slider for marking lengths. I find that I rely on my sewing gauge quite often—for marking hems, placing trim, and all manner of petite measuring tasks.

PINS & NEEDLES. Basic dressmaker's pins will be fine for your early projects. Later on, you may want to add thin silk pins or long quilter's pins (with perky colorful heads) to your stash of sewing supplies.

You'll do very little hand sewing for the projects in this book. An assortment of *sharps* (all-purpose sewing needles) is fine.

PINCUSHION. Store all of your pins and needles in a pincushion. You can get the ubiquitous tomato or the groovy felt orb, or perhaps try a magnetic pincushion. Lately I've come to favor the magnetic varieties because they can grab the pins that have misbehaved and escaped to the floor.

THREAD. All-purpose thread, which is cotton-wrapped polyester, is fine for any of the tops in this book. As your adventure in sewing continues, you may eventually want to use all-cotton thread (great for woven, natural fiber fabrics) or perhaps all-polyester thread (good for fiber blends and knits). When you're choosing a thread color for your top, either match it to the fabric or choose a shade that's slightly darker.

BODKIN. Sounds like something from Harry Potter, doesn't it? Actually, a bodkin is an ingenious tool used to thread elastic through a casing, as in the halter top on page 60. (For the thrifty, a big safety pin is a good alternative to using a bodkin; just pin it to the end of the elastic and feed it through the casing.)

MARKING TOOLS. Your pattern pieces will have some markings (circles, center points, darts, and the like) that need to be transferred to the fabric. There are several different ways you can accomplish this: with tailor's chalk or chalk pencil, with water-soluble or air-soluble (i.e., disappearing) fabric pens, or with tracing paper and a tracing wheel. You should always test your marking supplies on a scrap of your fabric before you begin to sew. We'll take some of these tools for a spin when we put them to use on page 27.

MISCELLANEOUS NOTIONS. In case you're interested, (and I'm sure you are), notions include all the other things you need to sew besides the pattern and fabric. We've already talked about the most important things you'll need, but here's a quick word about a few other items.

The projects begin with a couple of simple tops, including the halter top we just talked about, so you'll need some elastic for the back. We'll use a zipper, too. Many of the tops have *interfacing* somewhere or

Marking tools

another; interfacing is special fabric that's used to stabilize areas in your garment. The interfacing used in this book is fusible, which means that it bonds to the fabric with heat and pressure. Some of the tops may need a snap or a button or two.

IRON. You can't make a top (or anything else, for that matter) without an iron. Pressing is very important to set seams and, indeed, to the very success of your final product. Note that we're not talking about *ironing*, which is sliding your iron across the fabric. We're talking about *pressing*. Pressing is moving the iron across the fabric in increments by pressing it up and down. Press open each seam before it's overlapped or crossed by another seam. Remember—up and down, not side to side. Ironing can distort the grain of your fabric.

Learn to Sew!

Without further ado, or even a drumroll, let's begin to make that fabulous top. If the process of sewing has intimidated you before, maybe you ought to think about it as you would the process of cooking. You choose a recipe (the pattern); buy the ingredients (fabric and notions); do the washing and chopping (preparing and cutting out the fabric); and then add the ingredients to one another according to the recipe (sew by following the pattern instructions). See—a piece of cake. Or, if you'd rather—easy as pie!

I digress. Back to the topic at hand. Let's begin with the fabric.

Prepare the fabric

You have to know a little more about fabric to understand the importance of the proper layout and subsequent cutting of your top, so bear with me a moment. When we discussed fabric earlier, we talked about prewashing. Now, prewashing actually means shrinking, as many washable fabrics will do just that when laundered. Generally, the looser the weave, the more shrinkage is likely to occur. Washing also removes sizing or finishes that may affect the quality of your stitches. Check the label on the bolt of cloth for the laundering recommendations, and wash the fabric the same way you plan to launder the top. Please don't neglect this very important step, because you'll be totally bummed to wash your blouse for the first time and then find that it's way too small for you. After you've laundered your fabric, press it to remove any wrinkles.

These swatches each have a different type of selvage.

Align the grain

Your fabric must be correctly aligned before you cut out the pieces for your top, and here's why. (We'll get to the how in just a few minutes.) Woven fabric is made of lengthwise and crosswise threads. In a perfect world, the crosswise threads are perpendicular to the lengthwise threads. The direction of these threads is called the *grain*.

Your pattern pieces must follow the proper direction of the grain so your top fits correctly. Most garment pieces follow the lengthwise (or straight) grain, because the lengthwise threads are designed to be stronger to withstand the tension of the weaving process. (The same lengthwise/crosswise relationship is present in knits, too, but the lengthwise stitches are called *ribs*, and the crosswise rows are called *courses*.) Some of the tops in this book are cut along the *bias*; the bias flows along the diagonal between the lengthwise and crosswise threads. Garments cut on the bias have wonderful drape and cling to the body because this is the direction in which woven fabric has the most stretch.

The finished border on the length of the fabric is the *selvage*. This border differs in appearance from fabric to fabric. Most cutting layouts will have you fold the fabric lengthwise with the selvages aligned; then you'll smooth out the fabric so it's flat. If you can't get the wrinkles out and the fabric won't lie flat, you may need to straighten the crosswise edges and try again. Why? Sometimes the length of the fabric wasn't perfectly cut along a crosswise thread or course. If you're starting to get that creepy

home ec feeling, chill: this is easier than it sounds, I promise. To find a crosswise thread on a woven fabric, clip into the selvage and pull out a crosswise thread across the entire width of the fabric. Then, trim the edge even along this visible line, as you see so easily done below. Fold the fabric again, aligning the crosswise ends and the selvages; the ends and the selvages should be perpendicular to one another.

Knits, being knits, behave a little differently. Because of their construction, you can't pull a thread across the fabric. (It's all looped together, remember?) Instead, straighten the ends with a carpenter's square. Now that you're educated about fabric preparation, you're ready for the next step.

Straighten the fabric ends, as shown here.

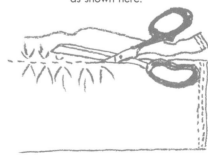

24

Prepare the pattern pieces

Grab your pattern and take out the pattern tissue and the instruction sheet. Look for your chosen design (let's say Top B), and you'll find a listing of all the pieces you need for Top B. Cut the pieces you need from the large sheets of tissue; be sure to cut out the

proper sizes. If you're using a multi-size pattern, which you probably are, you might want to highlight the cutting line for your size. To remove the wrinkles from the pattern pieces after you've cut them from the large pieces of tissue, press each piece with a dry iron set on low heat.

Let's look at the pattern pieces themselves for a moment. Some pieces will be cut on the fold, which will be indicated by a pair of arrows pointing to the edge of the pattern. These pieces are very easy to place correctly. Other pieces will be cut on the straight grain, indicated by a straight line with arrows on either end. These arrows must be parallel to the selvage so the fabric piece is cut on the straight grain. You insure this by measuring from each end of the arrow and adjusting until each end is the same distance from the selvage. Some pieces, such as facings, are often cut out from both fabric and interfacing, and this too will be indicated on the pattern piece. (A facing gets very lonely if you forget to cut its interfacing, so take note.)

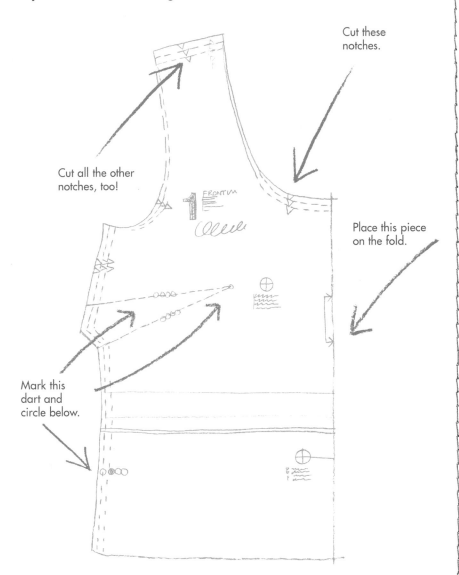

Cut these notches.

Cut all the other notches, too!

Place this piece on the fold.

Mark this dart and circle below.

Here's a typical top front. It has a couple of features that need to be marked, the dart and the circle. The arrows pointing to the edge indicates it will be cut on the fold. All the notches should be cut, as you need to match them when you make the top.

Fold the fabric

Find the cutting layout for Top B according to your size and your fabric width. Place your fabric on a flat surface and align it properly as discussed on the previous pages, following the directions in your pattern's cutting layout. Sewing gurus disagree on whether to fold the right side of your fabric (the face) to the inside or outside; sometimes you need to be able to see the pattern on the fabric, so the face should be on the outside. However, it's probably most convenient to fold the right side to the inside for a couple of reasons. First, it's easy to mark with the wrong sides outside, and second, the right sides need to be facing each other when you sew anyway. Before you start to pin the pieces to the fabric, place them all on the fabric to make sure you understand the layout.

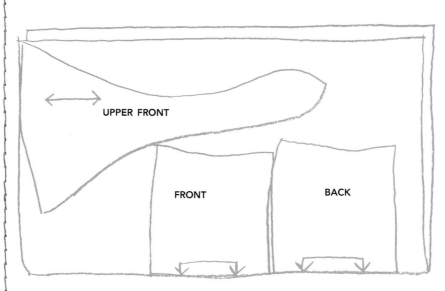

UPPER FRONT

FRONT

BACK

This is a typical cutting layout. As a matter of fact, it's the cutting layout for the Happy Halter, on page 60. The pieces that have arrows on the edges are cut on the fold, and the piece with the straight arrow is cut on the lengthwise (straight) grain. Remember to check your instructions carefully to make sure you cut the correct number of each piece.

Pin in place

Keep fiddling around with the pieces until the measurements agree and your piece follows the straight grain. Pin the grainline arrows and the foldline arrows in place first and then pin the edges of each piece, with the pins on a diagonal facing into the corners. Finally, pin around the edge of each piece. The sewing gurus also give some differing advice about pinning, but most suggest placing all the pins perpendicular to the cut edge. To begin, how about pinning them the way that's most comfortable for you? Pin all the pieces to the fabric and then refer to your layout to be sure you've placed each of the pieces for your top. After you're sure every piece is on the material, begin to cut. But not before!

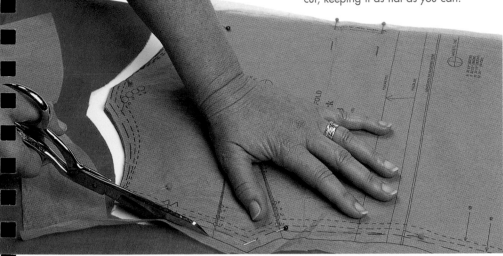

Lightly hold the fabric in place as you cut, keeping it as flat as you can.

Cut out the top

Keep the fabric flat as you work, holding the pattern piece in place with your free hand as you cut. The notches you see are important markers for you when you're making your top; these help you properly match the various pieces when you're stitching them together. While you can cut them outward, I've found that it can be tricky to keep the fabric flat while you navigate the scissors around them, so I generally zip right through the notches and cut them inward after I've cut the piece out. This method saves a little time, too. Be mindful that there are single, double, and even triple notches, so cut them as such. You'll match single notches to single notches, double notches to double notches, and so on.

Mark the fabric

Your pattern pieces may have marks such as circles, darts, or pleats that need to be transferred to the wrong side of the fabric. The simplest way to do this is to use dressmaker's tracing paper and a tracing wheel. Usually, you can mark both pieces at the same time,

unless the fabric is textured or heavyweight. Remove as few pins as possible to allow you to access the area you need to mark. Place the colored side of the paper to the wrong side of the fabric and trace over the markings with the wheel. If you're transferring straight lines, a ruler can be useful in accurately tracing the lines and keeping the pattern tissue in the proper position.

There are many tools to mark fabric. If you need to transfer only a dot, you can mark it with a fabric marking pen or chalk pencil. Be sure to test the markers on a scrap of fabric to be certain you can remove the marks, if necessary. Because you may sometimes have to mark a placement line on the right side of the fabric, it's important to test your markers.

Use a ruler as a guide when you mark a straight line.

Start to sew

Okay, girlfriends, we're ready to sew. I hope you're as excited as I am! We've chosen a pattern, purchased the fabric and notions, and cut out and marked the top. Read through the next section and promise me you'll sit down at the sewing machine and practice stitching before you get started. Remember to familiarize yourself with your sewing machine and its controls (did I already tell you this?), and set up your workspace so all your tools and materials are handy.

In the following section, we'll talk about the basic techniques that we've used in our tops. Don't try to remember everything at once, but read it through so you have a general understanding of the process. Later, in the Make a Top! section, you'll see how the techniques work in context when you make your blouse. We've presented them here with contrasting stitching so you can easily see what happens during

Stitching the bodice to the Bohemian Rhapsody top (page 74)

each step. Furthermore, we've used fabric that's similar (in some cases identical) to what we used for our tops (linen, and a linen/rayon blend), so you can see real-world examples of how these fabrics behave when they're sewn. This isn't airbrushed sewing we're doing here.

And you may notice real-world sewing in the Make a Top! section, too—fabrics fray when they're handled and some techniques (like gathering) put more stress on the fabric, so you'll probably see a thread or two. You'll see them on your own tops as well. Since you're learning, you shouldn't be overly stressed out about what the inside of your garment looks like, but do tidy up your top when you're done, trimming all the loose threads. This isn't work now—it's fun and you're just beginning. So plug in the machine, turn on the lights, and let's sew. If you need a refresher course when you're making your top, you can always flip back to these illustrated techniques.

Stitch a seam

To avoid boggling your mind unnecessarily, we've kept the sewing fairly simple in *Fun & Fabulous Tops*, using only basic techniques. There are three stitches: the *straight stitch*, the *basting stitch*, and the *zigzag*. The straight stitch is the foundation of your top; you can also do the straight stitch in reverse to anchor the beginning of your seams or to provide reinforcement at certain points, such as a zipper opening. (Consult our friend the manual for reverse stitching.) The basting stitch is simply a straight stitch set to a longer length. Use basting stitches to temporarily hold layers together or to gather fabric. Zigzag stitches are used to finish the raw edges of seams, or for just plain fun.

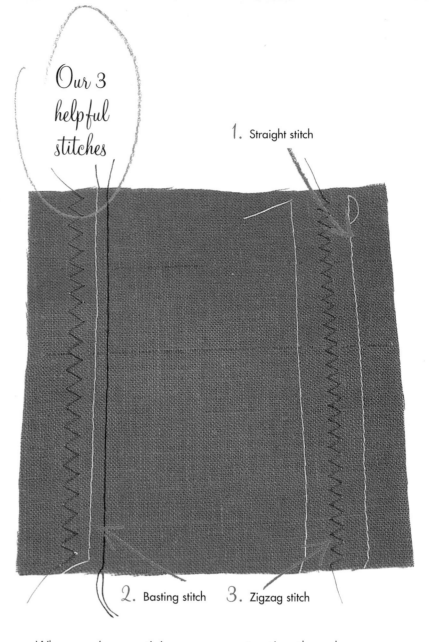

Our 3 helpful stitches

1. Straight stitch

2. Basting stitch   3. Zigzag stitch

When you're practicing, use a contrasting thread so you can easily see what's happening. Also, use two pieces of fabric for the best results; sewing machines are designed to join two layers of fabric, so the top and bobbin stitches meet in the middle. Refer to You Know What for the proper way to thread your machine, wind the bobbin, and accurately set the stitch length. A setting of 10-12 stitches per inch is average for garment sewing. If you're using a knit fabric, though, you

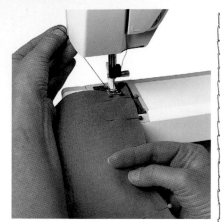

Gently hold the threads when you begin stitching.

may need a shorter stitch (i.e., more stitches per inch).

To sew a seam, align the fabric edges and pin them together with the pins perpendicular to the edge of the fabric, heads near the edge. Line up the fabric to the ⅝-inch guideline on your sewing machine's needle plate; ⅝-inch seam allowances are standard in garment sewing. Place the fabric underneath the needle just a tiny bit (oh, ¼ inch) from the end of the fabric. Lower the presser foot. (Do remember to do this because gnarly things happen if you forget). Hold the bobbin and top threads while you backstitch a couple of stitches to the end of the seam. Let go of the threads and stitch forward, pausing to remove the pins as you go. Don't, don't, *don't* be tempted to stitch over

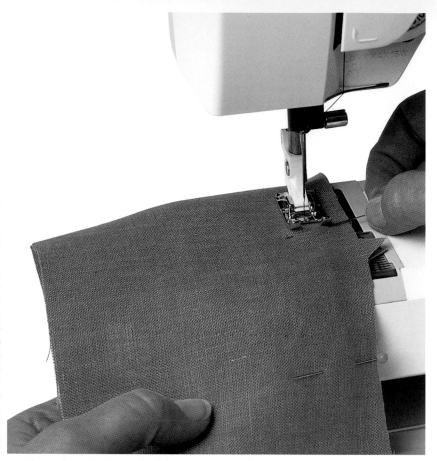

Let the machine do the work while you guide the fabric. Remove the pins before you reach them.

the pins—you can break a needle, or worse, ruin your machine's timing by hitting a pin. Or even worse, have shards of metal flying around you and your top.

Guide the fabric lightly with your hands, keeping it straight against the guideline on your needle plate. Watch the guideline and not the needle—it can be hypnotizing. (You may think I'm kidding, but I'm not!) Let the machine do the work of pulling the fabric along (that's what those busy little feed dogs do). When you reach the end of the seam, backstitch for a few stitches to secure.

Congratulations——you stitched your first seam.
Relax and have some chai.

Balance the tension

After your chai (need a snack, too?), take a moment to admire your first seam. Look at both sides of the fabric; the stitches should look nearly identical on each side, being locked between the two pieces of fabric. If they don't look identical, you may need to adjust the thread tension on your machine. Each thread (top and bobbin) has its own tension. You may need to make adjustments to the tension according to the type of fabric you're using to make your top. Every time you sew with a new fabric, you should check the tension first.

The examples at the right show correct tension; top tension that's too tight; and top tension that's too loose. When the top tension is too tight, it yanks the poor bobbin thread up to the right side of the fabric; the opposite happens when the top tension is too loose. Following the instructions in (guess what?) your manual, make small adjustments at a time and do test seams until you're happy with the tension setting.

To check thread tension, use different colors of the same thread—one color (black) on top, the other (white) in the bobbin.

The example above shows correct tension.

Here, the top tension is too tight.

This example shows top tension that's too loose.

Pivot

When you're sewing, you occasionally have to change direction—just like driving. When you need to do an about-face, you pivot the fabric like so: stop with the needle in the fabric. Raise your presser foot and turn the fabric. Lower your presser foot and have at it!

Trim seams and clip curves

At certain points along the way you'll need to trim a seam. Your pattern instructions will tell you when to do this. Generally, you trim a seam to reduce bulk in the finished garment (at the neckline of your top, for example). Simply use your shears to trim away the seam allowance to about ¼ inch.

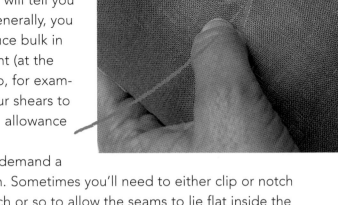

Curved seams demand a little extra attention. Sometimes you'll need to either clip or notch the curves every inch or so to allow the seams to lie flat inside the garment. You clip an inward curve by using the tips of the scissors to clip just to the seam. Be careful not to clip through the stitching, of course. On outward curves, cut notches from the seam allowance to eliminate fullness.

Guide the fabric

Sometimes, you don't need a complete change of direction, just some friendly guidance. Use a gentle pull of the fabric to keep the fabric aligned on your needle plate.

Clipping

Notching

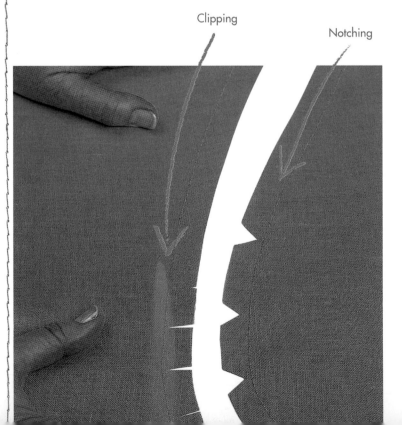

Finish the seams

To prevent raveling and make your top last longer, finish the exposed seam allowances. You can do this before or after you stitch the seam, depending on the method you choose. Let's talk briefly about the various finishes, starting with the before.

ZIGZAG. If you want to finish the seams before you sew, sew a line of zigzag stitching into the seam allowance, as close to the cut edge as you can. This is a good choice for fabrics that tend to ravel easily. After stitching the seam, press it open. If you're using a lightweight fabric, you might find that it's a little tricky to stitch into the single thickness without the fabric puckering, so use one of the methods that follow instead.

Now, to the after. The following methods can be used after the seam has been stitched.

DOUBLE-STITCHED. The double-stitched seam is suitable for lightweight fabrics and knits. After the seam has been sewn, stitch a parallel line of stitching in the seam allowance, then trim away close to the second line of stitching. Press to one side. (You could do a second line of stitching in a frisky little zigzag, too.)

PINKED. This is a good choice for tightly woven fabrics. Stitch about ¼ inch from the raw edge and then trim with pinking shears. Press open to finish.

After stitching together with the wrong sides facing, turn and stitch with the right sides together.

FRENCH SEAM. This is an enclosed seam that's perfect for sheer fabrics. Begin by stitching the *wrong* sides together in a 1/4-inch seam. Trim the seam to within a millimeter of its life (that is, very short) and turn the fabric inside out so the right sides are together. Now, stitch together in a 3/8-inch seam, encasing the raw edge. You've created a traditional-looking seam on the outside and a neat fold on the inside. You can use this method on straight seams only.

Here's a tidy fold on the inside, and a beautiful seam on the outside!

TOPSTITCH. To secure a seam allowance and provide a little pizzazz at the same time, trim one seam allowance to about 1/4 inch and press the remaining seam allowance over it.

On the outside, stitch about 1/2 inch from the seamline, catching the pressed seam allowance underneath.

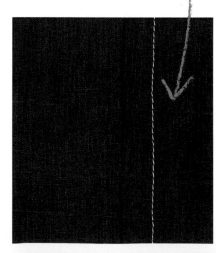

Right sides together

You'll almost always sew the pieces of your top with the right sides together (facing each other). This is the most basic fact you need to remember about garment sewing. If your fabric doesn't have easily recognizable right and wrong sides, be sure to mark each piece so you can quickly determine which is which, 'cause it's important.

Match notches

Remember when we cut the notches? Patterns include a series of notches to insure that you sew the correct pieces (and the correct sides of the correct pieces) to one another. If the notches don't seem to line up as the pattern instructions show, you may have one piece facing the wrong way, or you may be trying to make the wrong edge of a piece fit. The notches should match exactly. Studying your pattern carefully will help you understand the proper orientation of the pieces.

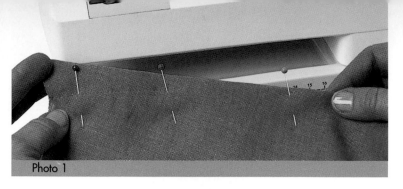

Photo 1

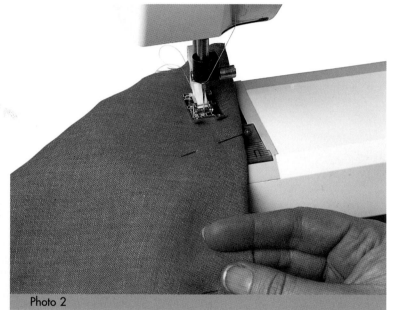

Photo 2

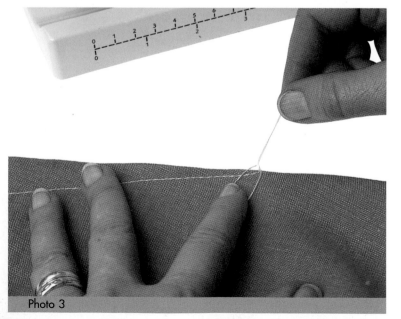

Photo 3

Staystitch

This will often be your first step in making a garment. *Staystitching* is simply a line of stitching sewn ½ inch into the seam allowance to stabilize the piece. Staystitching is usually done on pieces that have curves, such as the neckline or the armscye. (Isn't that a fancy word? It means armhole.) Staystitching is designed to be permanent (unlike most boyfriends).

Sometimes, you'll clip to a line of staystitching to allow one piece to fit another (as when you're making a round piece fit a straight edge, for example).

Make a dart

Darts shape a top so it conforms to your body, so darts are your friends. Stitching a dart often follows the staystitching step when you're making a top. If your pattern calls for a dart, mark it carefully. You'll see that there's a peak in the center of the dart; fold the fabric at the peak, matching any markings, and pin (photo 1). Stitch, beginning at the wide end of the dart (photo 2). When you get to the narrow end of the dart, take a few stitches at the fold, but don't backstitch. Backstitching prevents the dart from lying flat. Instead, cut the threads long enough to tie into a knot to secure the end of the dart (photo 3). Your pattern will tell you which direction to press the dart.

Ease to fit

Sometimes, to insure the proper fit or drape, you'll sew one piece to another that's ever-so-slightly longer. This is called *easing* or *easestitching*, created by gently gathering a portion of the longer piece until it matches the length of the shorter piece.

Easestitching is done with a row or two of basting stitches that are pulled to fit. Always stitch with the eased section face up. The fullness should be distributed in the seam allowance and not visible in the finished top.

Gathering is a similar technique, but the pieces are usually very different in length and the gathers are designed to be visible on the garment. (Think peasant skirt, if you dare.)

Make a narrow hem

Most of the tops in this book have edges that are finished with narrow hems. It's just like it sounds: a skinny little hem that's stitched in place on the machine. Typically they're made like this: Stitch ⅜ inch from the raw edge and press up along this line of stitching. Tuck under the raw edge to meet the stitching, forming a nice fold. Press and stitch in place along the fold.

Now, there's also a *very* narrow hem, which is great for sheer or lightweight fabrics. To make a very narrow hem, machine-stitch 1/2 inch from the raw edge. Turn under on the line of stitching and stitch close to the fold. Trim the fabric close to the stitching line. Turn under 1/8 inch, encasing the raw edge. Stitch the hem in place. Press.

Understitch the facings

A facing finishes an edge. Understitching is used primarily on facings to make them behave and stay out of sight on the inside of a garment. After the seam has been trimmed and clipped, press the seam allowance toward the facing. From the right side, stitch close to the seamline through all layers. After understitching, turn the facing to the inside.

Here's how the facing looks on the inside.

Add a lining

Just as facings finish an edge, a lining finishes the inside of a garment. Many blouses and jackets have areas that are lined (and some jackets are completely lined, but we're not going there). Sometimes the lining is cut from separate pattern pieces, but often it's cut from the same pieces as your top. Sometimes, the lining is constructed from a thinner fabric than the top.

Set in a sleeve

No hiding, now—sleeves are *not*, I repeat, *not*, difficult to install. I mean it! The important thing to do is to make sure that all your markings (dots, circles, notches, etc.) match and that you check the fit before you sew. Here's a typical construction for a set-in sleeve, the kind we have in this book.

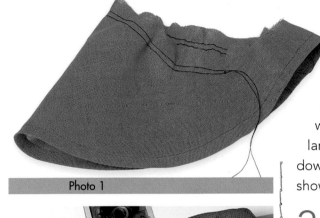
Photo 1

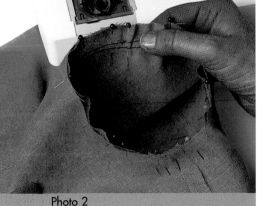
Photo 2

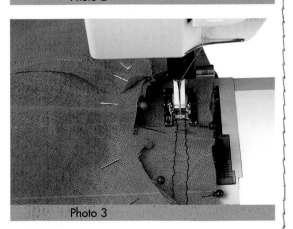
Photo 3

1 Prepare your sleeve as your pattern instructs; usually, this means adding a row of easestitching and maybe finishing the hem. Easestitching is usually done along the *sleeve cap* (the area that meets the shoulder and upper arm) so you can set the sleeve into the armscye (might as well use that fancy word again). Sleeves have to be a little larger than the opening so you can move your arm up and down. Our finished sleeve, complete with easestitching, is shown in photo 1.

2 Turn your top *wrong* side out. Turn the sleeve *right* side out, and place it inside the top. (The right side of the sleeve will be facing the right side of the top.) Manipulate the sleeve until the markings match and the ease is distributed properly. Pin in place (photo 2). With the sleeve side up, baste (photo 3). You should always set in a sleeve with the sleeve side up, so you can monitor the eased portion of the sleeve as you sew.

3 If this is your very first sleeve, you'll probably want to try on the top now and check the fit.

4 Stitch in place and trim the seam as instructed by your pattern.

See—I knew you could do it.

Isn't this a cool collar?

Add a collar

Eventually, you'll probably want to make a top that has a collar, just because. In traditional couture, collars are generally sewn onto the garment before the facings are added. In this book, just to be different, we feature a couple of edgy collars that are simply stitched on with no facings. Our enlightened collars are on pages 64 and 68; a more traditional collar is on the Sunday Jacket on page 98.

Install a zipper

Sooner or later—perhaps even this afternoon—you'll want to make a fitted top. Of course you've got to get into (and out of) said fitted top, so you might have to learn to install a zipper. A zipper is a wonderful device, so let's figure it out.

  There are several ways to put in a zipper, so how about we pick an easy one? The basic centered zipper is about as simple as it gets. You install a zipper in a seam that's partially sewn. Most patterns will have you stitch to a notch or a marked circle. Let's pretend that we've done that.

1 After stitching the seam to the appropriate spot, backstitch for a few stitches to anchor it. Now, baste the rest of the seam together and press it open. This is where the zipper goes.

Photo 1

2 Place the zipper facedown on the basted seam, with the zipper stop at the marked spot or notch. Put the zipper foot on your machine. Baste each side of the zipper in place, stitching the same direction (i.e., bottom to top) on each side (photo 1). Contrasting thread makes it easy to see the basting stitches when you have to remove them later on.

Photo 2

Photo 3

3 Reduce the stitch length to stitch your zipper in place. Begin at the seam below the zipper stop, stitch about 1/4 inch, pivot, and stitch up the side. Follow your basting stitches or mark your stitching line, if you prefer. Repeat on the other side (photo 2).

4 Remove the basting stitches along the sides of the zipper (photo 3). Finally, rip the basting stitches in the seam to reveal your zipper (photo 4). It's finished (photo 5). Isn't it beautiful?

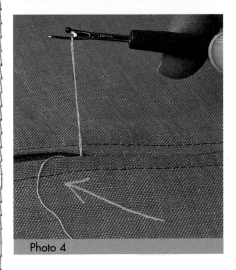

Photo 4

Photo 5

Stitch by hand

You only need a few basic hand stitches to complete these tops. A basic *hemstitch* can multitask to secure facings as well as to hem your top. A *tack* will hold facings to seam allowances.

Begin with a knot in your thread; make a simple loop in the end and pull the needle through. Sometimes a second knot is necessary to keep the thread from pulling through the fabric. A hemstitch is begun with the needle inserted into the fold of the fabric. Work from right to left as you pick up just a thread or two in the top and then insert the needle into the edge of the fold above the first stitch. Repeat, making stitches every ¼ inch or so.

Finish a line of hand stitching in one of two ways. Make a series of *backstitches* (a small stitch made from left to right and repeated several times in place). You can also make a quick knot. Make a wee stitch on top of your last stitch on the wrong side of your fabric, forming a small loop. Pull the needle through the loop until a second loop forms. Pull the needle through the second loop tightly to form a knot.

A tack is simply a straight stitch used to join layers of fabric; you can repeat them in place or make a series of straight stitches. You'll use them in your tops to anchor facings to seam allowances. Make sure your tacks don't go through the top itself, just the facings and seam allowances. You can also use the basic tack to sew a snap, a button, or a hook and eye in place.

Hemstitches in white thread; tacks in black thread; and backstitches in orange thread

Check the fit

Try on the top after each major step, such as when the side seams are sewn and the sleeves added. Don't wait until the blouse has been completed, because it will take a lot of sweat and even more tears to unmake it if you need to tweak the fit. Remember that it's better to err on the side of being too big than too small when you're deciding on a size. If you need to make the top smaller, do so in teeny increments, such as ⅛ inch. Exhibit A: If you're taking in the side seams, this seemingly tiny measurement translates into ¼ inch on each side of the top and ½ inch for the entire top.

If you're stressed about fit, use the traditional couture approach of making a *muslin*. A muslin is a sample garment that's made of inexpensive material (i.e., cotton muslin) for the purpose of testing the fit. The sample garment need only have the major pieces stitched together, with no seam finishes or completed details. A perk with making a muslin is that you can practice sewing before you begin your actual project. Then you're tweaking the muslin, and not your precious fabric. With a muslin, you'll be confident your top will fit after you've invested time and money in it.

A perfect fit!

Fix a mistake

The best way to fix a mistake is to avoid it in the first place. (Excuse me if I'm beginning to sound like your mother.) But of course, we all make them, even the most experienced seamstresses. There's not much that can't be repaired by simply ripping out all the stitches and trying again. When you're using a seam ripper to remove stitches, be careful not to tear the fabric by ripping too enthusiastically. I know how much fun it can be!

If you're having a weak moment and feel unsure about something you've just stitched, chill a second and make sure it's correct before you trim the seam allowances or clip the curves.

Photo 1

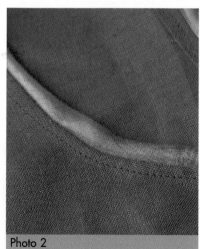

Photo 2

Photo 3

Embellish **Your Top**

Most of the tops you really love are likely to have some sort of embellishment—lovely ribbon, vintage lace, or whatever suits your fancy. Several of our projects are so decorated, and you can choose to include these embellishments as you wish. (But why wouldn't you? It's easy.) Even if your pattern doesn't call for trim or a decorative technique, you can still include them if you want. Here's the scoop on adding accoutrements to the tops, blouses, and jackets in this book.

We had a bit of fun inserting trim in seams, especially tulle. (If you always wanted to be a ballerina, like me, but couldn't quite pull it off, like me, here's your chance to indulge in a little fantasy.) We put tulle into exposed seams with raw edges (photo 1), but you can stick it anywhere—between any ol' facing and the thing it faces. There's a little bit of ribbon trim we inserted this way, too (photo 2).

If you're the vintage kind of girl, you'll have plenty of opportunities to add lace, rickrack, or fringe to your tops. You can add trim before you finish your top, or after. If you add trim before the top is complete (photo 3), the raw ends of the trim will probably be hidden inside a facing or turned to the inside with a seam.

If you add trim after the top is finished, you'll need to hide the raw ends of the trim, if you care about that kind of thing. When you cut the trim, remember to add an extra 1/2 inch or so for tidying the ends by folding them under. If you want a deconstructed look, simply add the trim without turning under the ends. What the heck.

Fabric itself can be used to create embellishments, too. One of our tops has a corsage sort of thing at the neck that is made from wavy strips of fabric stitched to the neck and tied (photo 4). You can also make a more traditional-looking fabric rose by simply gathering a long strip of fabric; when you cut it, trim the two ends of the edge you're not gathering into a gentle curve. Start at one end and roll the gathered edge into a bloom, stitching it together as you go.

You can also have a lot of fun combining fabrics to create visual interest. We paired black linen with hand-loomed silk for a shimmery contrast (photo 5). All we did was cut the pieces we wanted to highlight (the collar and the flounces) out of both fabrics, and trimmed one layer to reveal the other below. Beautiful. And easy.

Finally, there's embroidery. A few stitches can enliven just about any garment. You can follow the existing seamlines for a quick embellishment, or add more intricate work if that's your thing (photo 6). There are really cool flosses on the market now (rayon, silk, variegated, metallic, etc.) for your pleasure.

Because we like you so much, we've included some more techniques you can use to embellish your tops, blouses, and jackets on page 104. They're free with the purchase of *Fabulous Tops!*

Photo 4

Photo 5

Photo 6

Use This Book

Alright, people, we've discussed just about everything you really need to know about making a top. We've looked at how-to photographs and illustrations. I'm just about ready to turn it over to you. Here's how the projects in this book will help you make your own top when you're...

CHOOSING YOUR PATTERN. Because I think much of the fun is in finding the pattern, I won't insist that you use the same design we did in the projects that follow. Why not? Because patterns are tied to fashion trends just like ready-to-wear garments in stores, so the companies update their offerings and discontinue patterns as the market dictates—a perfectly reasonable business practice. To allow for changing trends, the instructions give you enough information to find a pattern that has similar features to the one we used (and you smart chicks will probably find patterns that suit you even better than the ones we used). We've included illustrations of the patterns we used on pages 108–110.

FOLLOWING THE INSTRUCTIONS. Purchase the fabric and notions as your pattern instructs. We'll give you the directions that we used to make our tops, including some tips and witty explanations for some of the techniques. (Commercial patterns assume that you have a basic knowledge of sewing, so sometimes a little extra information is oh-so-helpful.) Our illustrated how-to instructions will complement the directions in your pattern envelope. If your pattern has similar features to ours, the directions should be somewhat alike, too. The basic instructions in *Fabulous Tops* (such as setting in a sleeve or understitching a facing) should apply to just about any pattern that has similar construction.

ANALYZING OUR PROJECTS. Generally speaking, the tops are presented in categories according to ease of construction, beginning with a basic tank top. The icons will rate the ease of the pattern, and the key on page 49 explains which skills are included in each category. As the tops progress, techniques are added so you'll have gained a repertoire of sewing skills by the end of the book. Once you understand a technique—making a narrow hem, for example—you can apply it to any project. See pages 50 and 51 for a quick preview of each top.

PREPARING TO SEW. Now that you've got everything you need to begin sewing, arrange your tools and materials within easy reach. And there's nothing worse than squinting while you're sewing, so treat yourself to adequate lighting in your workspace.

   Speaking of tools and materials, you'll see a list for each of our top projects. However, we're not going to list every supply you need for each top, but rather refer you to this list of basic top-making tools and materials. Have the following on hand for any simply irresistible project in our Make a Top! section:

sewing machine

machine needles

measuring tools

marking tools

scissors

seam ripper

pins

needles for hand sewing

thread

Only a few more pages of handy information and we'll be ready to rid the world of top depression!

   Of course, you'll also need any additional notions suggested by your pattern.

Anatomy of a Top

Here's a quick visual recap of the top-making process.
Pretty simple, isn't it?

 +  + 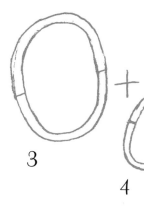 =

1   2   3   4   5

1 Staystitch the edges and make the darts in the front.

2 Stitch front to back at the sides and shoulders.

3 Add the facing and the trim to the neckline.

4 Add the facings to the armholes.

5 Hem the edges.

In the blink of an eye,
your own handmade top.
Wear with pride.

Icon Key

Each of our projects is rated according to ease of construction. (Please note that I didn't say *difficulty* of construction.) Here's how we've organized them.

ABSOLUTE BEGINNER
Suitable for the first-time sewer.

BASIC SKILLS YOU'LL USE:

Matching notches (page 35)

Narrow hem (page 37)

Right sides together (page 35)

Make a dart (page 36)

Ease to fit (page 37)

Understitch the facings (page 38)

Staystitch (page 36)

Trim seams and clip curves (page 32)

Handstitch (page 42)

Seam finishes (page 33)

EASY BEGINNER
Suitable for the new sewer who understands the basics and is ready to add sleeves.

NEW SKILLS YOU'LL USE:

Add a collar (page 40)

Set in sleeves (page 39)

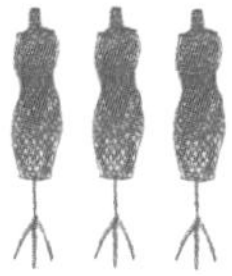

EXPERIENCED BEGINNER
Suitable for the sewer who's mastered the basics and is ready to sew at warp speed.

NEW SKILLS YOU'LL USE:

Install a zipper (page 40)

Add a lining (page 38)

Understitch (page 38)

Tip
A tip offers you a nifty idea.

Why?
Wondering why you're doing something? Here's the answer.

Runway Preview

Here's the scoop on the tops you'll see in our collection.

1 PRETTY IN PINK A fun tank top is transformed into something much more elegant with silk ribbon trim. It's easy to make and embellish.

2 SENSATIONAL SHRUG Don't tell anyone how easy this shrug is; it's only two pieces! Richly colored fabric makes it special.

3 HAPPY HALTER Classic seersucker goes just a little—dare we say it?—sexy in this terrific halter top with an elasticized back.

4 EDGY LITTLE TOP Yes, you can put in a sleeve. This easy top also has hip raw edges everywhere.

5 SATURDAY JACKET The fit of this easy jacket is created by its clever construction. Just wait and see!

6 BOHEMIAN RHAPSODY A delicate fabric and a winsome design combine to create a lovely sleeveless blouse with overlapping panels.

7 DAY OR NIGHT BLOUSE This versatile wraparound blouse can go anywhere, anytime. We dressed ours up with silk accents.

8 COMPLETELY COCO It's as chic as its namesake, pairing elegant silk fabric with deconstructed details.

9 TOTALLY TRIMMED Lining the bodice allows you to use sheer fabrics, and the trim allows you to have fun!

10 SUNDAY JACKET When you're heading uptown, instead of downtown, put on this smart jacket with traditional details. Here's a secret—it's made of upholstery fabric.

Now let's get busy & make a top!

Cash, check and charge.

Pretty in *Pink*

A little silk ribbon makes this simple top a bit more special.

WHAT YOU NEED

Pattern for a pullover tank top

Fabric and notions per the pattern envelope (we used linen, matching thread, and 1-inch variegated, hand-dyed ribbon)

Basic top-making tools and materials (page 47)

ABSOLUTE BEGINNER

Cheat sheet for absolute beginner on page 49

Pattern schematics on page 109

HOW YOU MAKE IT

1 Cut out and mark the top according to your pattern's instructions. Stitch the darts in the front (photo 1). Press down the darts.

2 With the right sides facing, pin and stitch the front and the back together at the shoulders. Right sides still facing, pin the front and the back together at the side seams, leaving the seams open below the large circles (photo 2). Stitch (photo 3).

Photo 1

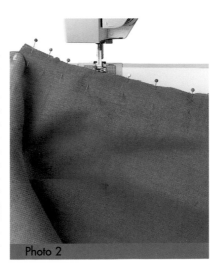

Photo 2

Photo 3

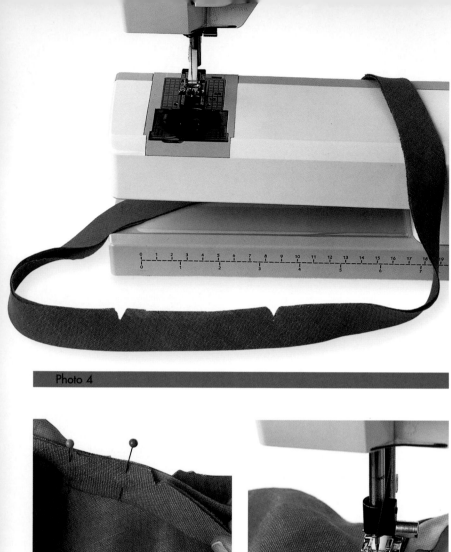

Photo 4

Photo 5

Photo 6

3 Staystitch the neck edge of the top; be sure to stitch in the direction your pattern indicates.

4 To finish the neck edge, you'll make a facing. To begin, stitch the ends of the neck facing, right sides together. With the wrong sides together, fold the facing in half; press lightly (photo 4).

5 Insert the ribbon between the neck facing and the neckline as you pin the neck facing in place, matching all notches and markings (photo 5). It doesn't matter which side of the facing you place against the neck edge—hurray! Stitch, stretching the facing to fit. Trim the seam and press it toward the facing.

6 Turn the facing to the inside along the seamline. Baste in place; it may help to use contrasting thread, so it's easy to see when you remove it. Stitch close to the basted edge (photo 6). Here's what the finished neck edge will look like (photo 7).

7 Staystitch the armhole edges; be sure to stitch in the direction your pattern indicates.

8 Prepare the armhole facing as you did the neck facing in step 4. (We didn't add ribbon trim here, but you certainly could if you wanted to.) Pin the facing to the armhole edge, placing the large circle at the shoulder seam. (Again, it doesn't matter which side you place against the top.) Stitch. Trim the seam and press it toward the facing.

9 Turn the facing to the inside, baste, and stitch in place as in step 6.

10 To finish the hem, turn up 1/4 inch on the raw edge and press. Now, turn up a 1-inch hem and press. Baste close to the fold and the upper edge. Topstitch the hem along the upper line of basting stitches (photo 8). Remove all the basting stitches.

11 Make a 5/8-inch narrow hem at the side opening edges, tapering to nothing above the large circles. Create the narrow hem by pressing under 5/8 inch, then tucking under the raw edge to meet the pressed fold. Stitch the hem in place, pivoting across the seam allowance about 1/4 inch above the large circle. Here's how this looks on the inside (photo 9) and the outside (photo 10).

Photo 7

Photo 8

Photo 9

Photo 10

Sensational *Shrug*

For a trip to the hottest new restaurant, please wear this stretch velvet shrug. Add a special bijoux to complete the look.

WHAT YOU NEED

Pattern for a shrug, designed for stretch knits only

Fabric and notions per the pattern envelope (we used polyester/spandex velvet, matching thread, and 1 hook and eye)

Basic top-making tools and materials (page 47)

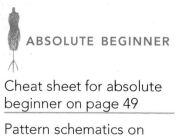

ABSOLUTE BEGINNER

Cheat sheet for absolute beginner on page 49

Pattern schematics on page 108

HOW YOU MAKE IT

1 Cut out and mark the top according to your pattern's instructions. With right sides together, pin and double-stitch the center back seam of the shrug, matching notches (photo 1).

Photo 1

How about
a booth?

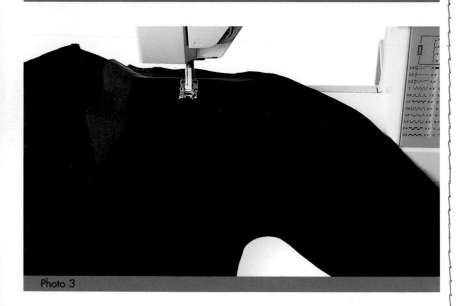

Photo 2

Photo 3

With right sides together, pin and double-stitch the front to the back at the shoulder and underarm seams, matching all the notches (photo 2). The shrug is almost finished (photo 3), in just the first step!

2 To make your first experience with knit fabric a happy one, use this simple method to finish the raw edges. Press or turn under the required hem on the neck edge of the garment; stitch in place along the edge (photo 4). Hem the front and lower edges of the shrug in a similar fashion.

3 Finish the sleeve hem as in step 2.

4 On the inside, sew a hook and eye to the front neck edge of the shrug (photo 5).

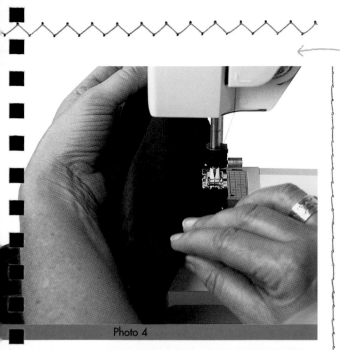
Photo 4

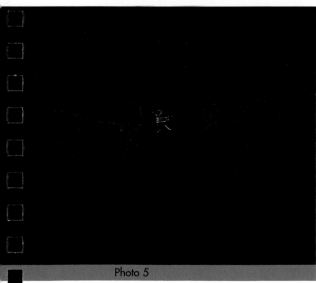
Photo 5

Why?

Knits don't ravel, so you don't have to be overly concerned with finishing the edges or the hem. Great, huh?

The word you're looking for is fabulous.

$\mathcal{H}appy$ Halter

How else to describe this easy top except fun?
Well, it's a little bit flirty, too.

WHAT YOU NEED

Pattern for a halter top with elasticized back

Fabric and notions per the pattern envelope (we used cotton seersucker, matching thread, and 1/4-inch elastic)

Basic top-making tools and materials (page 47)

Bodkin

ABSOLUTE BEGINNER

Cheat sheet for absolute beginner on page 49

Pattern schematics on page 108

HOW YOU MAKE IT

1 Cut out and mark the top according to your pattern's instructions. Finish the neck, ties, and armhole edges of the upper front with a narrow hem. Create the narrow hem by stitching 5⁄8 inch from the raw edge and pressing up along this line of stitching. Tuck under the raw edge to meet the pressed fold. Stitch the hem in place (photo 1).

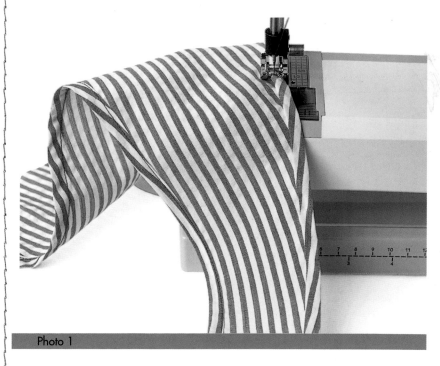

Photo 1

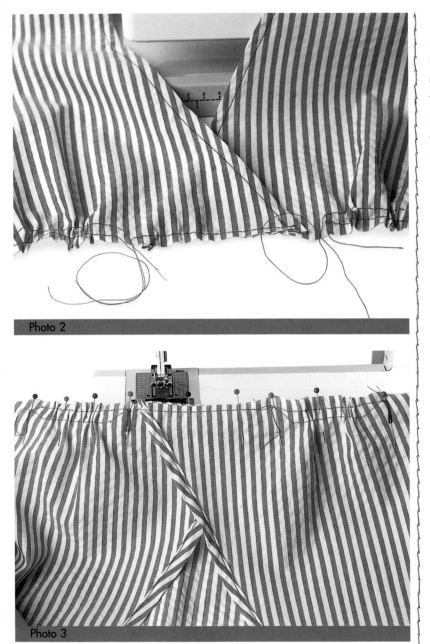

Photo 2

Photo 3

2 To gather the lower edge of the upper front between the notches, make two rows of basting stitches inside the seamline. On the outside, lap the right front over the left front, matching centers. With the raw edges even, baste across the lower edge (photo 2).

3 With right sides together, pin the lower front to the upper front, matching the centers and notches. Pull up the gathering stitches to fit. To secure the gathered section, wrap the long threads around the pins (photo 3). With the raw edges even, baste together, and then stitch. Press the seam toward the lower front. Note that the hemmed portion of the front will be placed at the seamline, not the raw edge (you'll see how this looks in photo 6).

4 To finish the back, you'll make a casing for the elastic. To begin, press under 5/8 inch on the upper edge of the back, turning it to the inside and forming the casing. Press under the raw edge 1/4 inch. Stitch close to the lower edge of the casing.

Photo 4

Photo 5

5 Cut a piece of elastic the length of the back elastic guide. Use a bodkin to insert the elastic through the casing (photos 4 and 5) until each end is even with the edge of the back. Stitch across the ends of the casing and the elastic. Pull out the ends of the elastic and trim close to the stitching.

6 With right sides together, pin and stitch the front to the back at the side seams (photo 6).

7 Stitch under the seam allowance diagonally at the upper edge of the side seam.

8 To finish the bottom edge, make a 5/8-inch narrow hem as in step 1. Here's the back of the finished top (photo 7).

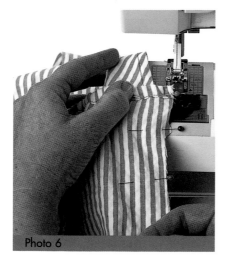

Photo 6

Photo 7

Edgy Little Top

Nothing's cooler than this clingy top with deconstructed details.

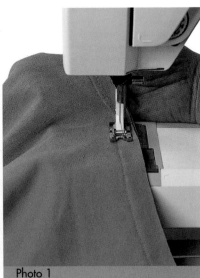

Photo 1

Photo 2

HOW YOU MAKE IT

1 Cut out and mark the top according to your pattern's instructions. With right sides together, pin and stitch the front and the back at the shoulders and the side seams, using double-stitched seams (photo 1). Press the seams toward the back.

2 Staystitch the neck edge of the top; be sure to stitch in the direction your pattern indicates.

3 Fold the ties in half to find the center. (See the tip on page 67.) With the right sides together, pin the ties to the neck edge (photo 2), centering them over the small marked circle at the right side. Baste the ties in place.

4 With right sides together, stitch the ends of the collar in a double-stitched seam. Press the seam toward the back.

WHAT YOU NEED

Pattern for a top with a collar and sleeves, designed for stretch knits only

Fabric and notions per the pattern envelope (we used cotton jersey and matching thread)

Basic top-making tools and materials (page 47)

EASY BEGINNER

Cheat sheet for easy beginner on page 49

Pattern schematics on page 108

I'm a Pisces—
and you?

5 Pin the *wrong* side of the collar to the *right* side of the top, (yes, that's correct), matching centers (photo 3). Clip the top neck edge if necessary. Stitch, and press the seam toward the inside of the top.

6 Topstitch the neck seam in place, keeping the outside ends of the ties free (photo 4). Trim the seam allowance close to the stitching.

7 With right sides together, stitch the sleeve in a double-stitched seam. Press the seam toward the sleeve back.

8 Now you'll set in the sleeve. With right sides together (and with the top turned inside out), pin the sleeve into the armhole, placing the large circle at the shoulder seam (photo 5); baste. Stitch (photo 6). Stitch again 1/4 inch into the seam allowance. Trim the seam close to the stitching. Press the seam allowances toward the sleeve.

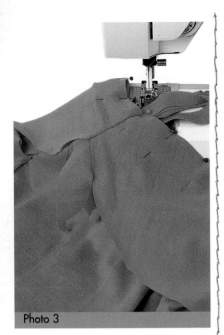
Photo 3

Photo 4

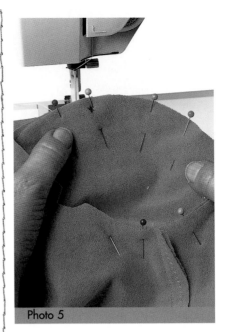
Photo 5

Photo 6

Photo 7

9 To wear your edgy top, make a knot or bow in the ties. Note that none of the raw edges are finished (photo 7).

Photo 8

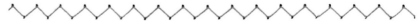

Tip

Instead of using a ribbon as our pattern called for, this designer created her own closure by simply cutting out four wavy pieces of fabric, grouping them together to form a funky corsage (photo 8).

I'll have something light and expensive.

Saturday Jacket

When you're feeling downtown and artsy, make this easy jacket with a ruffled collar and embroidery embellishment. Don't you dare finish the raw edges, either!

WHAT YOU NEED

Pattern for a short jacket with a ruffle or neck flounce

Fabric and notions per the pattern envelope (we used wool bouclé, matching thread, rayon embroidery floss, and perle cotton)

Basic top-making tools and materials (page 47)

Embroidery needle

EASY BEGINNER

Cheat sheet for easy beginner on page 49

Pattern schematics on page 109

HOW YOU MAKE IT

1 Cut out and mark the jacket according to your pattern's instructions. With right sides together, pin and stitch the front to the back along the underarm seams. This is how it will look (photo 1).

Photo 1

2 With right sides together, pin and stitch the notched ends of the sleeve flounces. Press both seam allowances to one side. Trim each of the under seam allowances to a scant 1/4 inch (photo 2).

Photo 2

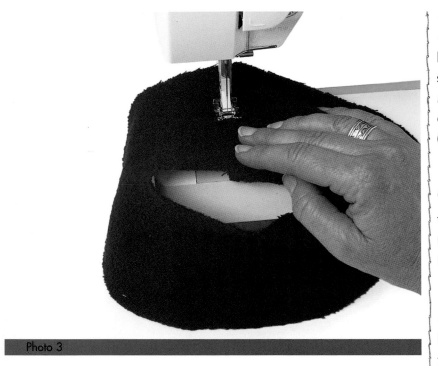

Photo 3

3 On the outside, topstitch 1/2 inch from the seamline, catching the untrimmed seam allowance. You'll find it's *much* easier to stitch from the outer edge to the inner edge (photo 3).

4 With right sides together, pin each sleeve flounce to the lower edge of each sleeve, matching the seams and the raw edges. Stitch (photo 4).

5 Trim the sleeve seam allowance *only* to within 1/4 inch of the stitching and press the seam toward the sleeve, pressing the sleeve flounce out. On the outside, topstitch each sleeve 1/2 inch from the seam, catching the seam allowance as in step 3.

6 With right sides together, stitch the center back seam of the collar and press both seam allowances to one side. Trim the under seam allowance to 1/4 inch. On the outside, topstitch 1/2 inch from

Photo 4

the seamline, catching the untrimmed seam allowance as in the earlier steps.

7 With right sides together, stitch the notched ends of the collar and the lower front and back sections together. Trim the lower front and back seam allowance *only* to within 1/4 inch of the stitching. Press the seam toward the lower front and back sections and topstitch 1/2 inch from the seamline. Here's what this piece will look like during this step (photo 5).

8 Pin the collar and lower front and back sections to the jacket, matching notches, centers and underarm seams, having the raw edges even (photo 6). Stitch the seam, occasionally lifting and curling the collar away from the stitching. This prevents the collar from having gathers at the stitching line. (See photo 8 of the Day or Night Blouse, page 83, for a picture of this technique.)

Photo 5

Photo 6

9 Trim the jacket seam allowance *only* to within 1/4 inch of the stitching. Press the seam toward the jacket, pressing the collar and lower front and back sections out. Topstitch the jacket 1/2 inch from the seam as in the earlier steps.

10 Embroider along the topstitching on the sleeves and jacket as desired. On our jacket, we used running stitch, French knots, and cross-stitch (photos 7 and 8), using rayon floss and perle cotton. Instructions for the embroidery stitches are on page 105.

11 If desired, add a line of zigzag stitching along the raw edges (photo 9). See the back of the jacket on the opposite page; this cool construction forms a cute little peplum effect.

Photo 7

Photo 8

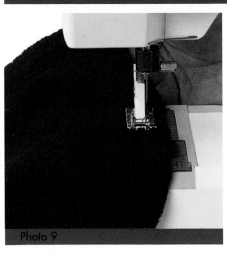

Photo 9

Tip
The wrong side of your fabric will show on the collar of this jacket, so make sure you like that side, too!

$\mathcal{B}$ohemian Rhapsody

A fabulous pattern calls for fantastic fabric—the result is perfect harmony.

WHAT YOU NEED

Pattern for a sleeveless blouse with lined bodice and asymmetrical hem

Fabric and notions per the pattern envelope (we used silk chiffon, rayon lining, matching thread, matching zipper, and 1 hook and eye)

Basic top-making tools and materials (page 47)

EXPERIENCED BEGINNER

Cheat sheet for experienced beginner on page 49

Pattern schematics on page 108

HOW YOU MAKE IT

1 Cut out and mark the blouse according to your pattern's instructions. Gather the lower edge of the upper front between the set of small marked circles on the left and right sides. For ease of viewing, the lining is shown here (photo 1); this is how the blouse should look at this stage, too.

Photo 1

2 With right sides together, fold each shoulder strap in half lengthwise. Stitch each long edge in a 3/8-inch seam.

3 Turn each shoulder strap right side out. Press. Baste raw edges together. Gather the ends of each shoulder strap and adjust the gathers to equal 1 inch. The strap is shown before and after gathering in photo 2.

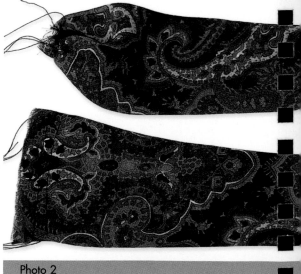

Photo 2

These guys are great live.

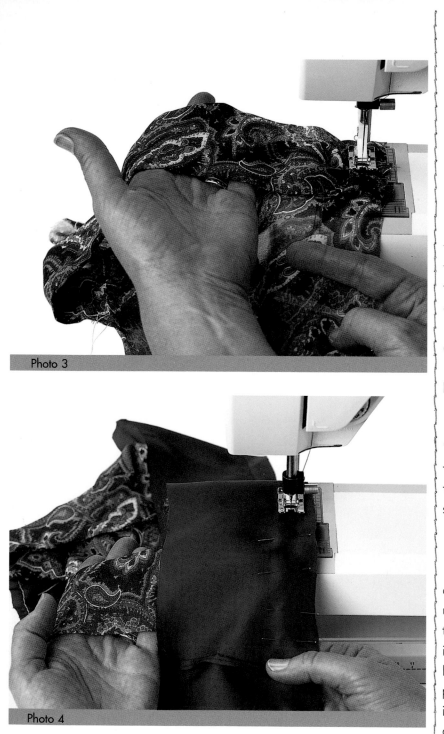

Photo 3

Photo 4

4   On the outside, pin each shoulder strap to the upper edge of the upper front, matching the marked circles. Baste the straps in place.

5   With right sides together, pin and stitch the upper front and the upper back together at the right side. On the outside, pin the remaining end of the shoulder strap to the upper edge of the upper back (photo 3), matching the markings. With the raw edges even, baste the straps in place.

6   Make the upper front lining in the same manner as the upper front, disregarding the straps. (Remember that this step is illustrated in photo 1.)

7   Pin the lining to the upper section, matching notches, centers, and seams. Stitch the upper edge (photo 4) and trim the seam. Understitch the lining: to understitch, press the lining away from the blouse and press the seam toward the lining. From the right side, stitch close to the seamline, through all layers of the seam allowance and the lining.

8 Turn the lining to the inside and press. Baste the lower edges and side opening edges together.

9 With right sides facing, stitch the right front and back sections together on the side with the notches (photo 5).

10 Make a 5/8-inch narrow hem or very narrow hem on the lower edge of the right front and back. To make a very narrow hem, machine-stitch 1/2 inch from the raw edge. Turn under on the line of stitching and stitch close to the fold. Trim the fabric close to stitching line (photo 6). Turn under 1/8 inch, encasing the raw edge. Stitch the hem in place. Press.

11 With right sides facing, stitch the left front and back sections together at the side seams, leaving the left side free above the large marked circle. Make a 5/8-inch narrow hem or very narrow hem on the lower edge of the left front and back as in step 10.

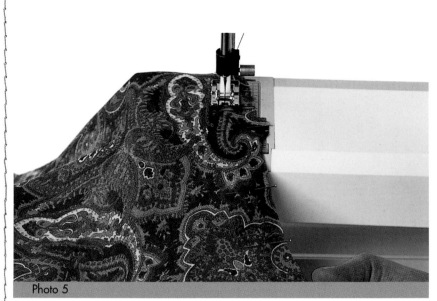

Photo 5

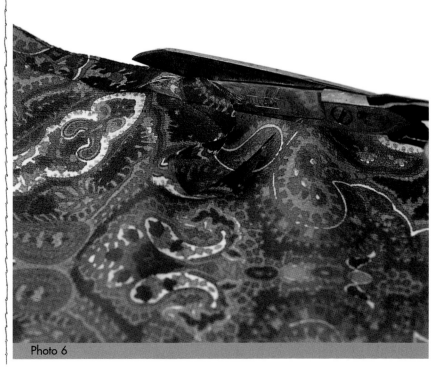

Photo 6

Tip

To tempt you, we've included a blouse made from this to-die-for chiffon. But you should use it only after you've gained a bit of sewing experience. Chiffon is all about me, me, me, and it must be treated delicately.

In an ideal world, it should be cut out on a non-slippery surface, such as felt, with the pattern pieces held in place with weights designed for that purpose. While sewing, use silk pins; set your machine to a light tension and a shorter-than-normal stitch length. The French seam technique is best for any long, straight seams.

If you're wary of using chiffon, remember that your pattern envelope will suggest a variety of fabrics for your skirt.

12 Pin the *wrong* side of the right front and back to the *right* side of the left front and back, matching notches, centers, and seams. Baste together (photo 7).

13 Pin the upper edge of the lower sections to the lower edge of the upper section, matching notches, marked circles, centers, and seams. Adjust the gathers to fit. Baste. Stitch (photo 8). Stitch again 1/4 inch away in seam allowance. Press the seam allowances toward the lower sections.

14 To install the zipper, begin by basting together the side opening edges along the seamline, above the marked circle. Press open the seam.

15 Place the closed zipper face down on the pressed seam allowance, placing the zipper stop at the marked spot and the zipper teeth on the seamline. Use the zipper foot to baste each side of the zipper in place (photo 9). Reduce the stitch length and install the zipper. Remove all the basting stitches.

16 Sew a hook and eye above the zipper.

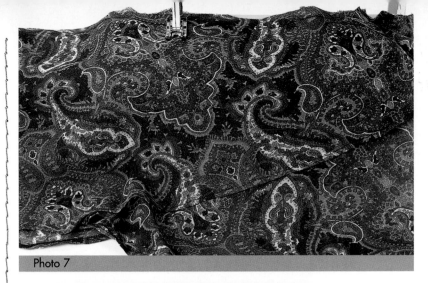

Photo 7

Photo 8

Photo 9

Day or Night Blouse

Wear this top anytime—dress it down with jeans, or dress it up with heels—just wear it. You won't be sorry.

WHAT YOU NEED

Pattern for a wrap-around blouse with flounces

Fabric and notions per the pattern envelope (we used linen/rayon embroidered fabric, hand-woven silk for the accents, matching thread, a snap, fusible interfacing, and grosgrain ribbon for the ties)

Basic top-making tools and materials (page 47)

EXPERIENCED BEGINNER

Cheat sheet for experienced beginner on page 49

Pattern schematics on page 110

HOW YOU MAKE IT

1 Cut out and mark the blouse according to your pattern's instructions. Stitch the dart in each bodice front. Trim to 5/8 inch and press each dart open (photo 1).

2 Cut 2 ribbon ties, each approximately 24 inches long. Baste one tie to the right front opening edge, matching the circles. Baste the remaining tie to the left front, matching the circles (photos 2 and 3).

Photo 1

Photo 2

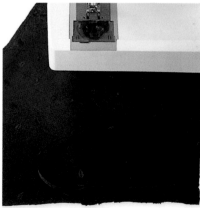

Photo 3

3 Stitch the darts in the bodice back and press them toward the center.

4 Easestitch the shoulder edges of the back between the notch and the neck seam allowance.

5 With right sides together, pin the back and front together at the shoulders. Adjust the ease, baste, and stitch (photo 4). Pin and stitch the back and front together at the side seams.

6 With right sides together, pin and stitch each front flounce to the back flounce at the side seams.

7 Staystitch the inner edge of the flounce; be sure to stitch in the direction your pattern indicates.

8 Make a 5/8-inch narrow hem on the front opening and lower edges, folding in the corners. Create the narrow hem by stitching 5/8 inch from the raw edge and pressing up along this line of stitching. Tuck under the raw edge to meet the pressed fold. Stitch the hem in place (photo 5).

Photo 4

Photo 5

Photo 6

Photo 7

Photo 8

9 Pin the flounce to the bodice, matching small circles, centers, and seams, clipping the flounce as necessary (photo 6). Baste. Stitch. Press the seam allowances toward the bodice.

10 Staystitch the neck edge of the blouse; be sure to stitch in the direction your pattern indicates.

11 To make this collar, we cut out a second collar piece from the silk fabric. Make both collars like so: stitch the collar sections together at the center back. Trim away 1 1/2 inches from the outer edge of the linen collar, marking as necessary. Baste the two layers together along the neck edge, with the linen collar on top of the silk collar. If desired, stitch the two layers together along the outer edge of the linen as well. We left the raw edges unfinished (photo 7).

12 Staystitch the notched edge of the collar; be sure to stitch in the direction your pattern indicates.

13 Pin the *wrong* side of collar to the *right* side of the garment, matching the notches, centers, and large circles, clipping the neck edge of the blouse as necessary. Baste in place (photo 8), occasionally lifting and curling the collar away from the stitching as shown. This prevents the collar from having gathers at the stitching line.

14 Fuse the interfacing to the wrong side of the bodice front facing and back neck facing, following the manufacturer's instructions. With right

sides together, pin and stitch the front and back facings together at the shoulders. Finish the long unnotched edge of the facing by turning under 1/4 inch, pressing, and stitching. Press under the seam allowance on the lower edges of the facing (photo 9).

Photo 9

15 Pin the facing to the front opening and neck edges (photo 10). Stitch and trim the seam. Understitch the facing and press it to the inside. Tack the facing to the seams and slipstitch the lower pressed edge of the seam.

16 Easestitch the upper edge of each sleeve between the notches. Easestitch the back edge of each sleeve between the notches.

17 With right sides together, pin the sleeve seam, matching notches. Adjust the ease, baste, and stitch.

18 To make the contrasting sleeve flounces, we cut two additional sleeve flounces out of silk. We reversed the order we used in step 11, and trimmed away 1 1/2 inches from the silk flounces. Place the silk flounce on top of the linen flounce and baste together along the edge of the silk, if desired. Slash each sleeve flounce along the solid line (photo 11).

Photo 10

19 With right sides together, stitch the seams in the sleeve flounces, matching notches and squares. We left the edges unfinished (photo 12).

20 Staystitch the inner edges; be sure to stitch in the direction your pattern indicates.

21 Pin each flounce to the lower edge of a sleeve, matching the markings and clipping the flounce as necessary. (See *Why?* on the next page). Baste, and then stitch. When you're working with a narrow circumference such as this sleeve, arrange the sleeve under the presser foot and stitch in small increments, rotating the sleeve as necessary (photo 13). Stitch again 1/4 inch away in the seam allowance. Trim close to the second line of stitching. Press the seams toward the sleeves.

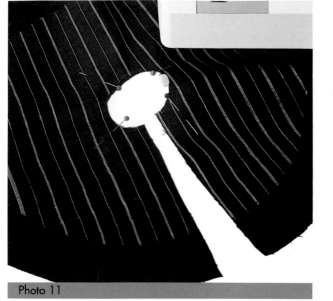

Photo 11

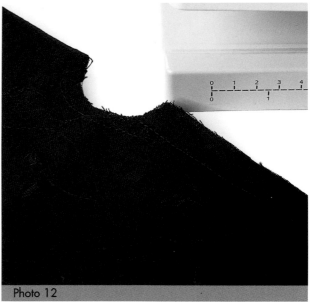

Photo 12

Photo 13

22 Now you'll set in the sleeve. With right sides together (and with the blouse turned inside out), pin the sleeve into the armhole, placing the marked circle at the shoulder seam. Adjust the ease, baste, and stitch. Stitch again 1/4 inch away in the seam allowance. Trim close to the second line of stitching. Press the seam allowance toward the sleeve.

23 To finish, add a snap. On the inside, sew the ball section of the snap to the right front at the marked spot (photo 14). On the outside, apply the socket section of the snap to the left front at the marked spot.

Photo 14

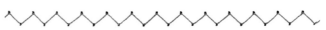

Why?
Clipping to the seamline enables you to spread the circular flounces to fit the cuffs, so the seamlines match.

Completely Coco

No wardrobe is complete without a jacket like this,
which mixes feminine tulle with trendy raveled edges.

WHAT YOU NEED

Pattern for an unlined jacket with pockets

Fabric and notions per the pattern envelope (we used silk tweed, contrasting thread, fusible interfacing, and matching tulle)

Basic top-making tools and materials (page 47)

EXPERIENCED BEGINNER

Cheat sheet for experienced beginner on page 49

Pattern schematics on page 110

HOW YOU MAKE IT

1 Cut out and mark the jacket according to your pattern's instructions. Staystitch the front neck edge; be sure to stitch in the direction your pattern indicates.

2 With right sides together, pin and stitch each front to a side front, matching the marked dots.

3 Now you'll make the pockets. Cut four pocket pieces from the silk tweed; you'll use these pieces to make two pockets. (If desired, apply fusible interfacing to the wrong side of two of the pocket pieces, following the manufacturer's directions). Cut a piece of tulle for each pocket that's roughly three times the length of the pocket and about 1 1/2 inches wide.

4 Fold the tulle in half widthwise and gather it to fit the pocket. Baste the pieces of tulle in place along the tops of two of the pocket pieces (photo 1). Now, place the

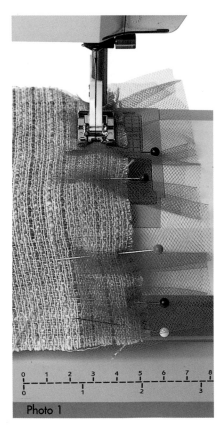

Photo 1

Thanks!
I worked really hard
for this promotion.

Photo 2

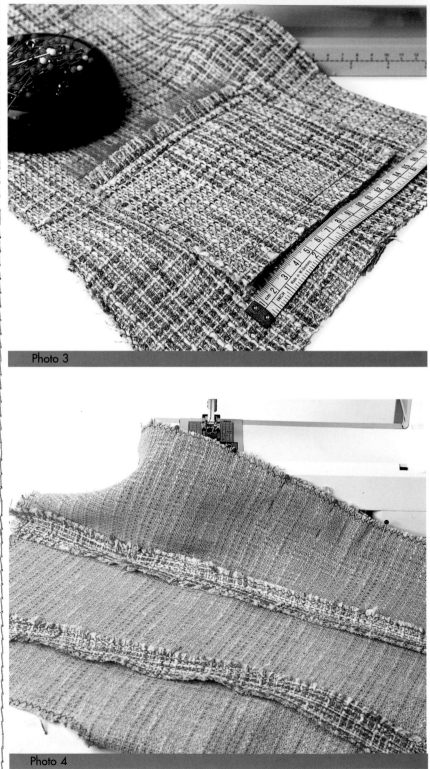

Photo 3

Photo 4

remaining pocket pieces on top of the pieces with the tulle, with the wrong sides together (photo 2). Pin in place and baste together around all the edges.

5 On the outside, place the pockets on the front along the marked line (photo 3). Pin in place. Stitch close to the sides and lower edges of the pockets.

6 Staystitch the back neck edge as you did the front in step 1. With right sides facing, pin and stitch together the center back seam of the back sections; pin and stitch the back to the side back sections (photo 4); and stitch the front to the back at the shoulder and side seams.

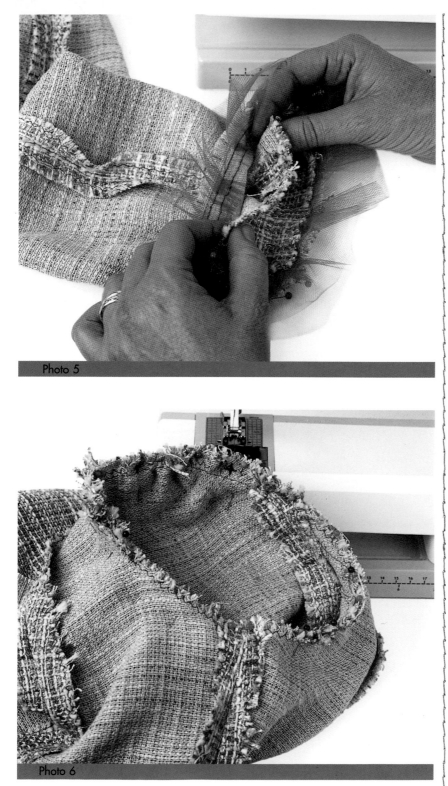

Photo 5

Photo 6

7 With right sides together, pin each upper sleeve to an under sleeve, matching the notches. Stitch the front and back edges. Easestitch the top of the sleeve between the notches.

8 If desired, apply fusible interfacing to the wrong side of the sleeve facing, following the manufacturer's directions. With right sides together, stitch the ends of each sleeve facing. Cut pieces of tulle to insert in each cuff, using the formula from step 3 (three times the circumference x 1$\frac{1}{2}$ inches). With the *wrong* sides together, stitch the facing to the lower edge of sleeve, inserting the tulle as you did in step 4 (photo 5). Turn each sleeve right side out.

9 Now you'll set in each sleeve. With right sides together (and with the jacket turned inside out), pin the sleeve into the armhole, placing the marked dot at the shoulder seam and matching all remaining marked dots. Pull up the easestitches to fit (photo 6). To distribute the fullness evenly, slide the fabric along the easestitches until there are no puckers or tucks on the seamline.

Baste. Stitch. Stitch again 1/8 inch from the first stitching. Trim the seam below the notches close to the stitching line. Press *only* the seam allowance, shrinking out any fullness.

10 Pin the fusible interfacing to the wrong side of the front and the back facing sections. Trim diagonally across any corners that will be enclosed within the seams. Fuse the interfacing in place following the manufacturer's instructions. With right sides facing, stitch together the front and back facing sections at the shoulder seams.

11 With right sides together, pin the facing to the jacket, matching centers and shoulder seams. Stitch along the seamline on the neck edges of the facing *only*. Trim the seam and turn the facing to the inside.

12

Cut pieces of tulle to insert along each front edge, using the formula from step 3 (three times the length x 1½ inches). Pin and stitch the front and lower edges together (the wrong sides will be facing) along the seamline, inserting the tulle in the front edges as in step 1 (photo 7). Trim all the tulle accents as desired (photo 8).

Tip

For this jacket, we used the pattern for inspiration and added our own touches—the tulle and the raw-edge finish. If you like raw edges, you can use this idea of applying the facings with the wrong sides together to create this look. You can also insert any type of trim that extends from the raw edges to the seamline, as we did here. Let your muse guide you.

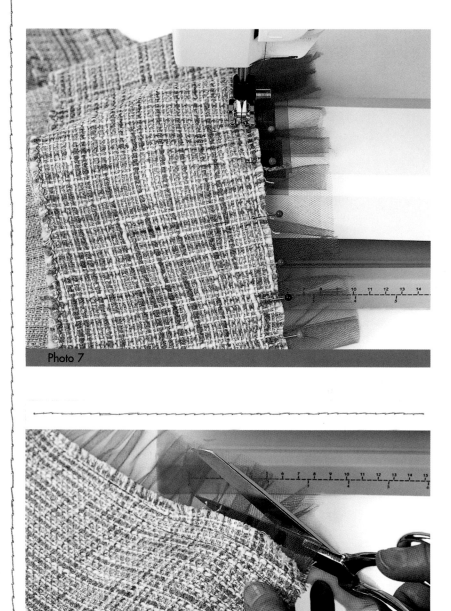

Photo 7

Photo 8

Totally Trimmed

Mod fabric and retro trim combine to create a thoroughly contemporary blouse.

WHAT YOU NEED

Pattern for a short-sleeved blouse with a V-neck and trim

Fabric and notions per the pattern envelope (we used synthetic crepe, matching thread, and vintage lace)

Basic top-making tools and materials (page 47)

EXPERIENCED BEGINNER

Cheat sheet for experienced beginner on page 49

Pattern schematics on page 109

HOW YOU MAKE IT

1 Cut out and mark the blouse according to your pattern's instructions. Staystitch the bodice front and back neck edges; be sure to stitch in the direction your pattern indicates.

2 With right sides together, pin and stitch the bodice front to the back at the shoulder seams (photo 1).

Photo 1

3 With right sides together, pin and stitch the shoulder seams of the bodice front lining and back facing sections. Finish the unnotched edge of the back facing by turning under 1/4 inch, pressing, and stitching with straight or zigzag stitch (photo 2).

4 With right sides together, pin the lining and facing to the bodice front and back, matching centers and shoulder seams, having the raw edges even. Stitch the front and back edges ending at the large marked dot; backstitch at the dot to reinforce the seam. Trim the seam and clip the curves (photo 3).

Photo 2

Photo 3

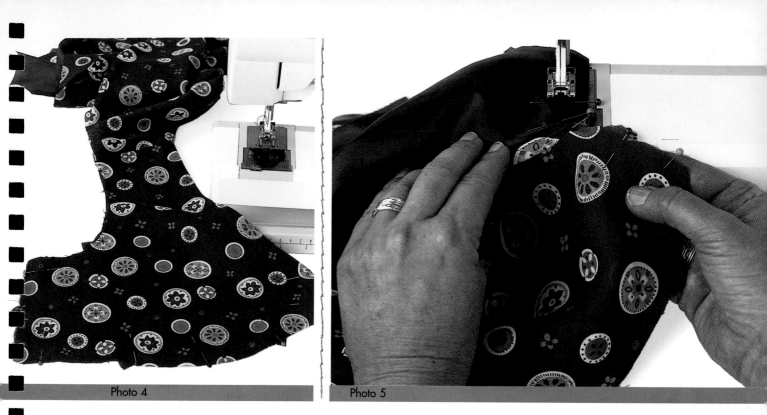

Photo 4

Photo 5

5 Turn the lining to the inside. Pin the lining in place and press (photo 4).

6 Open out the bodice and lining at the center front. With right sides together, pin the bodice and lining along the center front seam, matching seams and markings. Stitch the center front seam between the marked dots (photo 5). Backstitch at the dots to reinforce the seam. Trim the seam.

7 Turn the bodice front to the outside. Press (photo 6).

8 Baste the lower and side edges of the bodice front as pressed, wrong sides together. Gather the lower edge of the bodice between the notches.

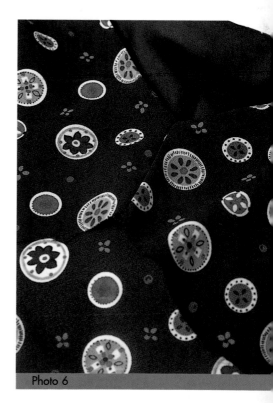

Photo 6

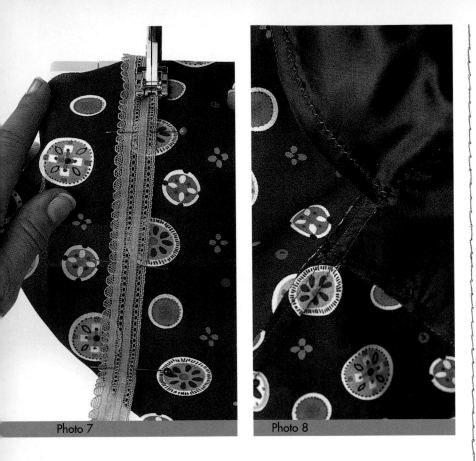

Photo 7

Photo 8

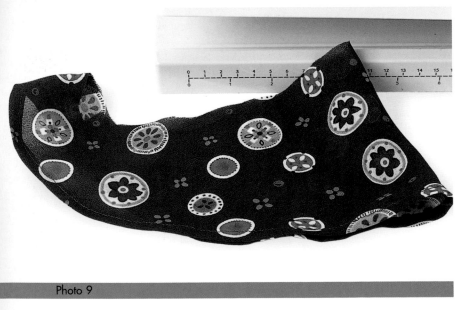

Photo 9

9 Pin the lace along the placement lines on the front. Stitch close to one or both edges of lace (photo 7). Baste the cut edges of the lace to the raw edges of the blouse, trimming any excess lace as necessary.

10 With right sides together, pin the bodice front to the front, matching centers and markings. Pull up the gathering stitches to fit. Baste. Stitch the seam, pivoting at the center marking. Press the seam toward the front.

11 With right sides together, pin the front to the back at the side seams. Turn the upper edge of the back facing over to the front. Stitch the front to the back at the side seams. Clip the front side seam allowance below the facing. Turn the facing to the inside. This is how this part of the blouse looks when it's finished (photo 8).

12 Stitch the underarm seam of each sleeve, right sides together. To make a very narrow hem, stitch 1/4 inch from the raw edge. Turn

under on the line of stitching and stitch close to the fold. Trim the fabric close to the stitching line. Turn under 1/8 inch, encasing the raw edge. Stitch the hem in place. Press. Turn the sleeves right side out (photo 9).

13 Now you'll set in each sleeve. With right sides together (and with the blouse turned inside out), pin the sleeve into the armhole, placing the marked dot at the shoulder seam, matching the underarm seams and remaining marked dots. Baste. Stitch. Stitch again 1/8 inch from the first stitching. Trim the seam below the notches close to the line of stitching.

14 Make a 5/8-inch narrow hem at the bottom edge. Create the narrow hem by stitching 5/8 inch from the raw edge and pressing up along this line of stitching. Tuck under the raw edge to meet the pressed fold. Stitch the hem in place.

15 On the outside, starting at the center back, pin the lace trim along the neckline as far as the center front. To form the miter at the center front, fold the lace back over

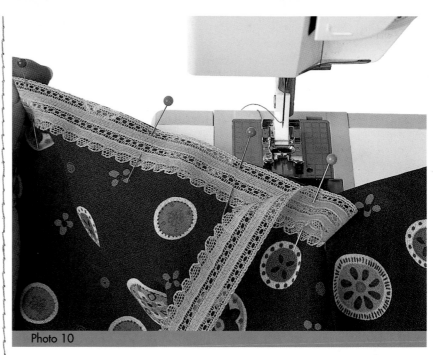

Photo 10

the portion you've already pinned to the garment (photo 10). Make a dart at the center, remove the pins from the neckline as necessary, and stitch the dart.

16 Continue pinning the lace to the neckline. Stitch close to the neckline edge, pivoting at the center front. Here's the finished trim (photo 11).

Photo 11

97

Sunday Jacket

When you're feeling elegant and refined,
put on this jacket with luscious velvet accents.

WHAT YOU NEED

Pattern for an unlined jacket with a collar and cropped sleeves

Fabric and notions per the pattern envelope (we used upholstery fabric, matching thread, matching velvet, covered buttons, 3 heavy-duty snaps, and 1 small snap)

Basic top-making tools and materials (page 47)

EXPERIENCED
BEGINNER

Cheat sheet for experienced beginner on page 49

Pattern schematics on page 109

HOW YOU MAKE IT

1 Cut out and mark the jacket according to your pattern's instructions. Staystitch the front and back edges; be sure to stitch in the direction your pattern indicates. Easestitch the side edge of the front between the notches.

2 With right sides together, pin each front to a side front. Pull the easestitches to fit. Baste (photo 1), and then stitch. Press the seams toward the front.

Photo 1

98

Let's get
this party started!

3 With right sides together, stitch the center back seam. Pin each back to a side back. Stitch the seams (photo 2). Press the seams toward the side back.

4 With right sides together, pin and stitch the front to the back at the shoulder seams. Pin and stitch the side seams.

5 Apply fusible interfacing to the wrong side of the under collar, following the manufacturer's directions. Stitch the center back seam of the under collar sections.

6 Apply interfacing to the wrong side of the upper collar as you did in step 5. With right sides together, pin the upper collar to the under collar, matching centers and marked dots. Stitch, easing the upper collar to fit and leaving the single notched edges open. Trim the seam; notch the curves (photo 3).

7 Turn the collar right side out. Press. Baste the raw edges together.

8 Clip the garment neck edge to the line of staystitching along the curves. With right sides together, pin the collar (under-collar-side

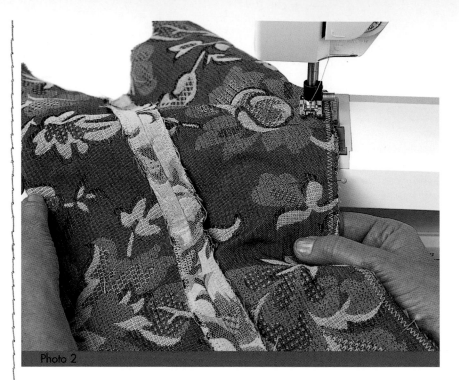

Photo 2

Photo 3

Photo 4

Photo 5

down) to the neck edge, matching centers, placing the small marked dots at the shoulder seams and the large marked dots at the center front (photo 4). Baste in place.

9 With right sides together, stitch the shoulder seams of the front and back facing sections. Finish the side edge of the front facing and the lower edge of the back facing by turning under 1/4 inch, pressing, and stitching with straight or zigzag stitch.

10 With right sides together, pin the facing to the jacket, matching centers and shoulder seams (photo 5).

11 Stitch across the facing exactly 1 1/4 inch above the lower edge, then 5/8 inch from the front and neck edge. (The stitching at the lower edge will help form the hem when the facing is turned to the inside.) Trim the facing below the stitching at the lower edge, trimming to within 5/8 inch of the inner edge of the facing. Trim the seam and corners; clip the curves.

12 Understitch the facing: to understitch, press the facing away from the jacket and press the seam toward the facing. From the right side, stitch

Photo 6

close to the seamline through all layers of the seam allowance and the facing.

13 Turn the facing to the inside; press, pressing up the hem we talked about in step 11. Baste the facing to the armhole edge. Finish the raw edge at the bottom by turning under 1/4 inch, pressing, and stitching with straight or zigzag stitch. Use a hemstitch to secure the hem.

14 Easestitch each sleeve between the notches. With right sides together, stitch each underarm seam to the marked dot.

Photo 7

15 Finish the lower edge of each sleeve with zigzag stitching. Turn the hem allowance to the outside, matching the large marked dots. Pin and stitch the ends in the 5/8-inch seam (photo 6). Trim the seams.

16 Turn the hem to the inside; press (photo 7). Stitch close to the inner pressed edge. Turn the lower edge to the outside, and fold to form a cuff (photo 8).

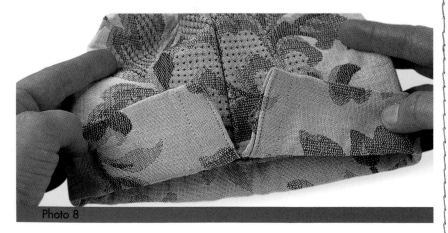

Photo 8

17 Now you'll set in each sleeve. With right sides together (and with the jacket turned inside out), pin the sleeve into the armhole, placing the marked dot at the shoulder seam and matching underarms seams and all remaining marked dots. Pull up the easestitches to fit. To distribute the fullness evenly, slide the fabric along the easestitches until there are no puckers or tucks on the seamline. Baste. Stitch. Stitch again 1/8 inch from the first stitching. Trim the seam below the notches close to the stitching line. Press *only* the seam allowance, shrinking out any fullness.

18 To make covered buttons, use fabric scraps and follow the buttton manufacturer's directions (photos 9 and 10). Sew the buttons to the right front at the marked dots.

19 Sew the knob portions of the heavy-duty snaps to the inside of the right front facing, under the buttons. Sew the socket portions to the outside of the left front at the marked dots (photo 11). Sew the knob portion of the small snap to the inside of the right front at the upper corner of the jacket. Lap the right front over the left, matching centers, and sew the socket portion of the small snap to the outside of the left front.

Photo 9

Photo 10

Photo 11

Tip

We used upholstery jacquard for this jacket, so it didn't need any additional interfacing. Because this fabric has a great deal of body, we also used rayon lining for the front of the jacket, instead of jacquard, to reduce bulk.

Embellishment Techniques

Here's your special bonus section—an overview of some simple embellishment methods you can use for your tops.

Sewing Techniques

Some of the stitches in this section and the embroidery section are interchangeable, as they can be used in dressmaking or embroidery.

APPLIQUÉ. The applying of one fabric layer to another. You can stitch appliqués by machine or by hand, using practically any of the stitches described in this section.

BLANKET STITCH. This loop stitch can be decorative or functional. After anchoring the thread near the fabric edge from the wrong side, insert the needle from the right side so it's perpendicular to the fabric edge. Pass the needle over the thread and pull, repeating for each successive stitch (figure 1).

SATIN STITCH. In machine stitching, make a satin stitch with zigzag stitch set to a short length, so the stitches are very close together. For hand stitching, see page 105.

TOPSTITCH. Done by machine on the right side of the garment, topstitching follows an edge or a seam.

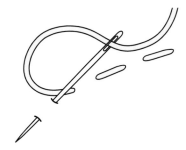

Figure 1. Blanket stitch

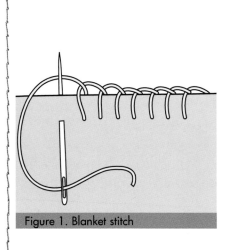

Figure 2. Running stitch

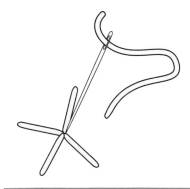

Figure 3. Straight stitch

104

Embroidery Techniques

Embroidery is an age-old embellishment technique. The tools and supplies you need for hand embroidery are few: floss, needles, an embroidery hoop, and perhaps a marking tool or quilter's tape. Usually, you'll want to separate the floss so you're working with three or fewer strands. Here are some basic embroidery stitches.

RUNNING STITCH. An easy stitch to execute, the running stitch is simply made by weaving the needle through the garment at evenly spaced intervals (figure 2).

STRAIGHT STITCH. Use a series of straight stitches to create a motif (figure 3).

SATIN STITCH. Satin stitch is composed of parallel rows of straight stitches (figure 4).

CROSS-STITCH. Cross-stitch is a series of diagonal stitches. The finished stitches can be touching one another or separated by space, as desired (figure 5).

FRENCH KNOTS. The elegant French knot is created by wrapping the thread around the needle once or twice (or thrice!), then inserting it back into the garment at the point where the needle emerged (figure 6).

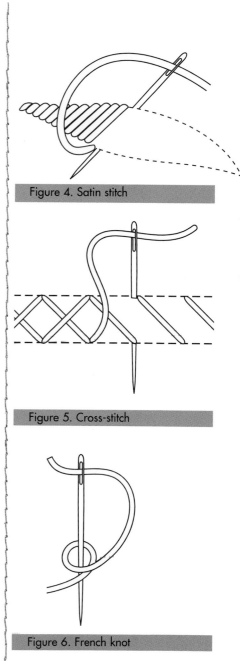

Figure 4. Satin stitch

Figure 5. Cross-stitch

Figure 6. French knot

Glossary

ARMSCYE. The armhole of a garment.

BACKSTITCH. A stitch worked from left to right; each new stitch ends at the left side of the previous stitch.

BASTING STITCH. A long, straight stitch used to hold pieces together temporarily or to gather.

BIAS. The diagonal between the lengthwise and crosswise threads in woven fabric. Fabric has the most stretch in this direction.

BODICE. The part of a garment that's above the waist.

CASING. A channel of fabric created to contain elastic or cording.

COURSE. The crosswise rows in a knitted fabric.

DART. A construction technique to create shape and fit in a garment.

EASE. This term has two different meanings. In sewing, ease means to adjust the length of one piece to fit another; ease-stitching with basting stitches is used when joining two pieces that are slightly unequal in length. In fashion, ease is the amount of sizing added to patterns to allow movement or for design purposes.

EASESTITCHING. *See ease.*

FACING. A separate piece of fabric used to finish an edge; in this book, a neckline might be finished with a facing.

FLOUNCE. A circular ruffle that isn't gathered to fit.

FREE ARM. A narrow sewing surface created when a removable accessory tray is detached from the sewing machine.

GATHER. To adjust the length of one piece to fit another; as opposed to easestitching, where the lengths of the pieces are only *slightly* different, the lengths of pieces that are gathered are *very* different. Usually, gathers are a design element in a garment.

GRAIN. The direction of the threads in woven fabric.

HEMSTITCH. A hand stitch that catches a thread of the garment and a thread of a folded edge.

INTERFACING. A special fabric that's used to stabilize parts of a garment.

MUSLIN. A copy of the garment with major seams sewn together. A muslin is designed to test fit.

NARROW HEM. A narrow folded hem stitched into place by hand or machine.

NOTIONS. All the other items you need to sew in addition to the pattern and the fabric.

PEPLUM. A flounce or garment extension at the hips.

PIVOT. To turn the fabric to change direction while sewing. Pivot by stopping with the needle in the fabric, lifting the presser foot, and turning the fabric.

PRESS. To move the iron across the fabric by pressing it up and down, as opposed to sliding it.

RIB. The lengthwise stitches in a knitted fabric.

SEAM ALLOWANCE. This is the amount of space between the edge of the fabric and the seamline. In garment sewing, ⅝ inch is the standard seam allowance.

SEAMLINE. The stitching line.

SELVAGE. The finished border on a length of fabric.

SLEEVE CAP. The portion of a sleeve that fits the shoulder or upper arm.

STAYSTITCHING. A line of stitching sewn ½ inch into the seam allowance to stabilize the piece.

STRAIGHT STITCH. The basic sewing machine stitch.

TACK. A straight stitch to join interior layers of fabric, such as a facing to a seam allowance.

UNDERSTITCHING. A line of stitching close to a seam that's designed to keep a piece in place. Facings are often understitched, for example.

ZIGZAG. A machine stitch in which the needle moves from side to side as it sews.

Designer Biographies

Kelledy Francis is an artist and seamstress working on her own line of fashion. She is currently obsessed with drafting a pattern for the perfect jeans. Kelledy holds a B.F.A. in fiber arts from the Maryland Institute, College of Art, and an M.F.A. in integrated media from Western Carolina University. She lives and works in Asheville, North Carolina, as a custom clothier and garment alterations specialist. See Kelledy's tops on pages 64 and 98.

Alexis Gault lives in Asheville, North Carolina, where she designs and sews original clothing for her company, Lush Life Designs. Alexis creates a fun, functional line of clothing designed to make the modern woman feel fabulous about her body. For more info, go to www.ilovelushlife.com. Her shrug is featured on page 56.

Glenda Larsen has been sewing clothes, home, and craft projects for 40 years. (Yikes!) She was taught to sew by her grandmother on an ancient treadle sewing machine. Glenda is the accounting manager at Lark Books and lives with her three cats on a mountain in Asheville, North Carolina. Glenda's blouse is on page 92.

The artistic endeavors of *Joan K. Morris* have led her down many successful creative paths, including ceramics and costume design for motion pictures. Joan has contributed projects for numerous Lark books, including *Hip Handbags* (2005), *Exquisite Embellishments for Your Clothes* (2006), and *Sew Cool, Sew Simple: Stylish Skirts* (2006). Joan's tops are on pages 60 and 74.

Nathalie Mornu has made projects for lots of Lark books, including *Hip Handbags* (2005), *Exquisite Embellishments for Your Clothes* (2006), and *Sew Cool, Sew Simple: Stylish Skirts* (2006). She lives in Asheville, North Carolina, but looks for shiny things wherever she may be. See Nathalie's tops on pages 80 and 86.

Pattern Schematics

To give you some perspective on the patterns we used, here are drawings of the pieces in each design.

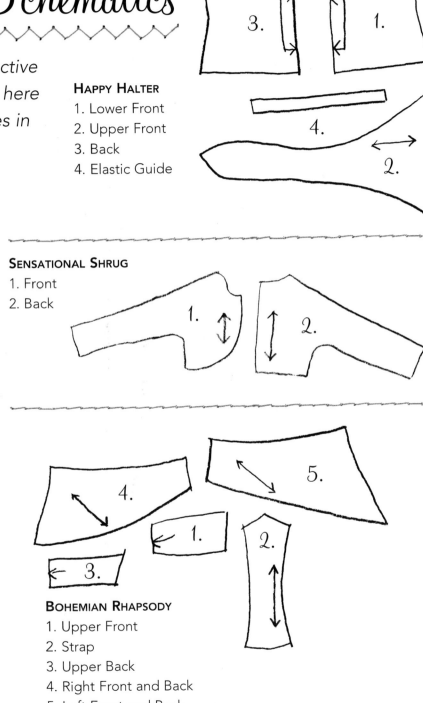

HAPPY HALTER
1. Lower Front
2. Upper Front
3. Back
4. Elastic Guide

SENSATIONAL SHRUG
1. Front
2. Back

BOHEMIAN RHAPSODY
1. Upper Front
2. Strap
3. Upper Back
4. Right Front and Back
5. Left Front and Back

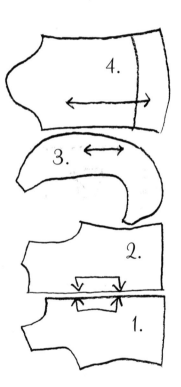

EDGY LITTLE TOP
1. Front
2. Back
3. Collar
4. Sleeve

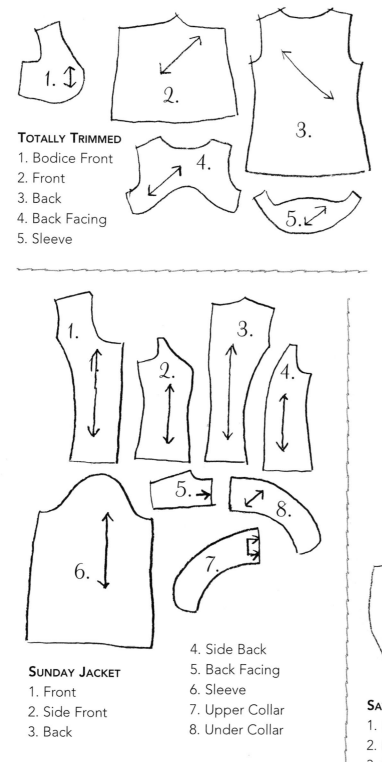

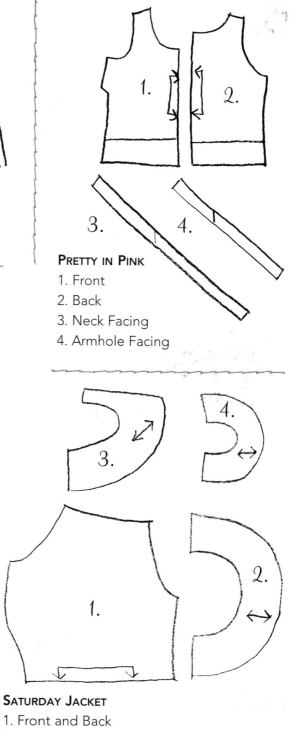

TOTALLY TRIMMED
1. Bodice Front
2. Front
3. Back
4. Back Facing
5. Sleeve

PRETTY IN PINK
1. Front
2. Back
3. Neck Facing
4. Armhole Facing

SUNDAY JACKET
1. Front
2. Side Front
3. Back
4. Side Back
5. Back Facing
6. Sleeve
7. Upper Collar
8. Under Collar

SATURDAY JACKET
1. Front and Back
2. Lower Front and Back
3. Collar
4. Sleeve Flounce

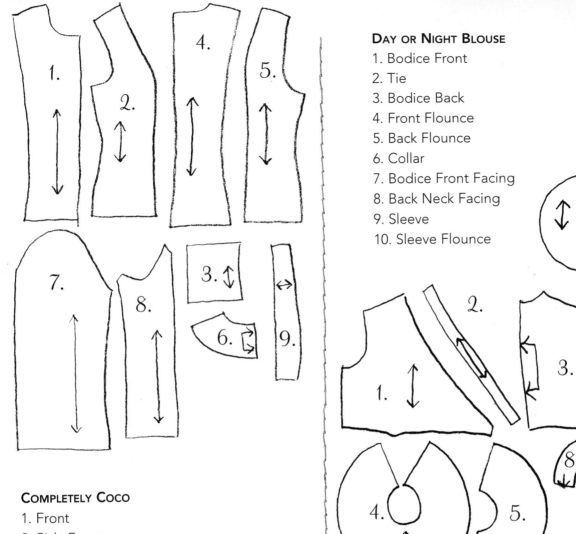

DAY OR NIGHT BLOUSE

1. Bodice Front
2. Tie
3. Bodice Back
4. Front Flounce
5. Back Flounce
6. Collar
7. Bodice Front Facing
8. Back Neck Facing
9. Sleeve
10. Sleeve Flounce

COMPLETELY COCO

1. Front
2. Side Front
3. Pocket
4. Back
5. Side Back
6. Back Facing
7. Upper Sleeve
8. Under Sleeve
9. Sleeve Facing

A Note About Suppliers

Usually, the supplies you need for making the projects in Lark books can be found at your local craft supply store, discount mart, home improvement center, or retail shop relevant to the topic of the book. Occasionally, however, you may need to buy materials or tools from specialty suppliers. In order to provide you with the most up-to-date information, we have created a list of suppliers on our website, which we update on a regular basis. Visit us at www.larkbooks.com, click on "Craft Supply Sources," and then click on the relevant topic. You will find numerous companies listed with their web address and/or mailing address and phone number.

Metric Conversion Chart

INCHES	MILLIMETERS (MM)/ CENTIMETERS (CM)
⅛	3 mm
3⁄16	5 mm
¼	6 mm
5⁄16	8 mm
⅜	9.5 mm
7⁄16	1.1 cm
½	1.3 cm
9⁄16	1.4 cm
⅝	1.6 cm
11⁄16	1.7 cm
¾	1.9 cm
13⁄16	2.1 cm
⅞	2.2 cm
15⁄16	2.4 cm
1	2.5 cm
1½	3.8 cm
2	5 cm
2½	6.4 cm
3	7.6 cm
3½	8.9 cm
4	10.2 cm
4½	11.4 cm
5	12.7 cm
5½	14 cm
6	15.2 cm
6½	16.5 cm
7	17.8 cm
7½	19 cm
8	20.3 cm
8½	21.6 cm
9 (¼ yard)	22.9 cm
9½	24.1 cm
10	25.4 cm
10½	26.7 cm
11	27.9 cm
11½	29.2 cm
12	30.5 cm
12½	31.8 cm
13	33 cm
13½	34.3 cm
14	35.6 cm
14½	36.8 cm
15	38.1 cm

INCHES	MILLIMETERS (MM)/ CENTIMETERS (CM)
15½	39.4 cm
16	40.6 cm
16½	41.9 cm
17	43.2 cm
17½	44.5 cm
18 (½ yard)	45.7 cm
18½	47 cm
19	48.3 cm
19½	49.5 cm
20	50.8 cm
20½	52 cm
21	53.3
21½	54.6
22	55 cm
22½	57.2 cm
23	58.4 cm
23½	59.7 cm
24	61 cm
24½	62.2 cm
25	63.5 cm
25½	64.8 cm
26	66 cm
26½	67.3 cm
27	68.6 cm
27½	69.9 cm
28	71.1 cm
28½	72.4 cm
29	73.7 cm
29½	74.9 cm
30	76.2 cm
30½	77.5 cm
31	78.7 cm
31½	80 cm
32	81.3 cm
32½	82.6 cm
33	83.8 cm
33½	85 cm
34	86.4 cm
34½	87.6 cm
35	88.9 cm
35½	90.2 cm
36 (1 yard)	91.4 cm

Index

Pattern Credits

The patterns used on pages 52, 64, 74, and 80 are courtesy of The McCall Pattern Company, 11 Penn Plaza, New York, New York 11215.

The patterns used on pages 56, 60, 68, 86, 92, and 98 are courtesy of the Simplicity Pattern Co. Inc., 2 Park Avenue, 12th Floor, New York, New York 10016.